Euthanasia

Editor: Tracy Biram

Volume 362

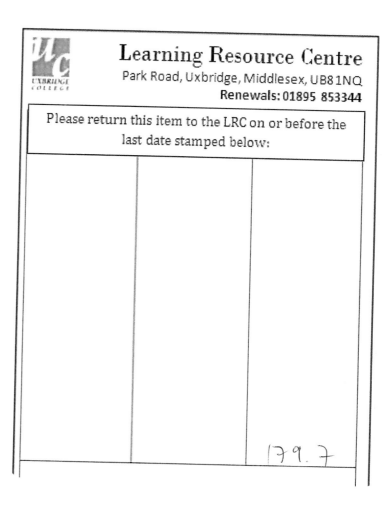

Independence Educational Publishers

First published by Independence Educational Publishers

The Studio, High Green

Great Shelford

Cambridge CB22 5EG

England

© Independence 2020

Copyright

Photocopy licence

ISBN-13: 978 1 86168 819 4

Printed in Great Britain

Zenith Print Group

Contents

Introduction

Euthanasia is Volume 362 in the **ISSUES** series. The aim of the series is to offer current, diverse information about important issues in our world, from a UK perspective.

ABOUT EUTHANASIA

The right to die topic is a highly sensitive, ongoing debate. Everyone has an opinion on this controversial subject. An increasing number of countries are legalising euthanasia and assisted suicide, this book explores the issue from both legal and ethical viewpoints.

OUR SOURCES

Titles in the **ISSUES** series are designed to function as educational resource books, providing a balanced overview of a specific subject.

The information in our books is comprised of facts, articles and opinions from many different sources, including:

- Newspaper reports and opinion pieces
- Website factsheets
- Magazine and journal articles
- Statistics and surveys
- Government reports
- Literature from special interest groups.

A NOTE ON CRITICAL EVALUATION

Because the information reprinted here is from a number of different sources, readers should bear in mind the origin of the text and whether the source is likely to have a particular bias when presenting information (or when conducting their research). It is hoped that, as you read about the many aspects of the issues explored in this book, you will critically evaluate the information presented.

It is important that you decide whether you are being presented with facts or opinions. Does the writer give a biased or unbiased report? If an opinion is being expressed, do you agree with the writer? Is there potential bias to the 'facts' or statistics behind an article?

ASSIGNMENTS

In the back of this book, you will find a selection of assignments designed to help you engage with the articles you have been reading and to explore your own opinions. Some tasks will take longer than others and there is a mixture of design, writing and research-based activities that you can complete alone or in a group.

FURTHER RESEARCH

At the end of each article we have listed its source and a website that you can visit if you would like to conduct your own research. Please remember to critically evaluate any sources that you consult and consider whether the information you are viewing is accurate and unbiased.

Useful Websites

www.blogs.bmj.com

www.care.org.uk

www.dignityindying.org.uk

www.equalityhumanrights.com

www.finalchoices.co.uk

www.independent.co.uk

www.inews.co.uk

www.legalcheek.com

www.nhs.uk

www.ridleyhall.co.uk

www.righttolife.org.uk

www.scotsman.com

www.standpointmag.co.uk

www.telegraph.co.uk

www.theguardian.com

www.thenational.scot

www.theosthinktank.co.uk

www.thestudentlawyer.com

www.theweek.co.uk

www.unherd.com

www.yougov.co.uk

Euthanasia and assisted suicide

Euthanasia is the act of deliberately ending a person's life to relieve suffering.

For example, it could be considered euthanasia if a doctor deliberately gave a patient with a terminal illness drugs they do not otherwise need for their comfort, such as an overdose of sedatives or muscle relaxant, with the sole aim of ending their life.

Assisted suicide is the act of deliberately assisting or encouraging another person to kill themselves. If a relative of a person with a terminal illness obtained strong sedatives, knowing that the person intended to use the sedatives to kill themselves, they may be considered to be assisting suicide.

The law

Both euthanasia and assisted suicide are illegal under English law.

Assisted suicide

Assisted suicide is illegal under the terms of the Suicide Act (1961) and is punishable by up to 14 years' imprisonment. Trying to kill yourself is not a criminal act.

Euthanasia

Depending on the circumstances, euthanasia is regarded as either manslaughter or murder. The maximum penalty is life imprisonment.

Types of euthanasia

Euthanasia can be classified as:

◆ Voluntary euthanasia, where a person makes a conscious decision to die and asks for help to do so

◆ non-voluntary euthanasia, where a person is unable to give their consent to treatment (for example, because they're in a coma) and another person takes the decision on their behalf, often because the ill person previously expressed a wish for their life to be ended in such circumstances.

Active and passive euthanasia

You may have heard the terms 'active euthanasia' and 'passive euthanasia'.

'Active euthanasia' is sometimes used to refer to deliberately intervening to end someone's life – for example, by injecting them with a large dose of sedatives.

'Passive euthanasia' is sometimes used to refer to causing someone's death by withholding or withdrawing treatment that is necessary to maintain life.

It's important not to confuse 'passive euthanasia' with withdrawing life-sustaining treatment in the person's best interests. Withdrawing life-sustaining treatment because it's in the person's best interests can be part of good palliative care and is not euthanasia.

29 June 2017

Euthanasia: the history & the law

The current law

The Suicide Act 1961 makes it an offence in England and Wales to assist someone if they commit suicide. Assisted suicide is punishable by up to 14 years' imprisonment; however, committing an offence does not automatically result in prosecution.

The Director of Public Prosecutions (DPP) has to consider whether a prosecution is in the public interest and in February 2010, published guidelines that set out the criteria under which someone would be prosecuted should they be charged with assisting a suicide. However, following her appointment, in October 2014 the DPP – Alison Saunders – rewrote part of the guidance, leading some to claim that 'doctors can now be involved in assisting suicide with almost no fear of prosecution, provided they don't have a professional relationship with those they "help".' This is clearly a matter of considerable concern.

This set up has resulted in an arrangement with respect to assisted suicide which the eminent former judge and Crossbench Peer, Baroness Butler-Sloss has described in the following terms: 'We have a law with the "teeth" to deter and the discretion, where appropriate, to temper justice with mercy.'

Assisted suicide in the courts

There have been many attempts to liberalise the law on assisted suicide in the courts over the years, all made by patients with terminal and life-degenerating diseases. The judiciary have always taken a deferential stance and argued that any changes to the law must be introduced by parliament.

Most recently in June 2018, Noel Conway argued that the current ban on assisted suicide under the 1961 Suicide Act (amended 2009) was incompatible with his human rights. However, the Court of Appeal reasserted that the current law is fair and balances the interests of wider society with the interests of individuals with terminal illnesses.

Supreme Court ruling 2018

In July 2018, the UK Supreme Court ruled that doctors would be able to withdraw food and fluids from brain-damaged patients with persistent vegetative state (PVS) and minimally conscious state (MCS) without needing to apply to the Court of Protection. These patients have food and fluids administered by tube (known as clinically assisted nutrition and hydration, or CANH), but can breathe without the assistance of a ventilator.

Prior to the Supreme Court's ruling, such patients had the ability to have their cases heard by the Court of Protection, which offered independent scrutiny of applications. As Dr Peter Saunders, director of Care not Killing argues, this was because the court 'recognised the emotional and financial pressure that families and clinicians can fall under.'

This judgement sets a dangerous precedent by removing safeguards for vulnerable patients, who cannot advocate for themselves. People with PVD and MCS might live in such a state for many years and some may regain a degree of awareness. By withdrawing CANH, these patients will very likely be starved or dehydrated to death under the auspices of their 'best interests'. Such a decision may be influenced by external factors such as the cost implications of continuing CANH or an ideological vested interest in withdrawing treatment.

The judgement also found that there is no essential difference between withdrawing food and fluids and switching off a ventilator – both are considered forms of medical treatment, as opposed to basic good care. According to Dr Saunders, there is a *'clear difference between turning off a ventilator on a brain-dead patient and removing CANH from a brain-damaged patient. PVS and MCS differ from conditions with a "downward trajectory" because they are not progressive and do not in themselves lead inevitably to death.' There are also 'demonstrable and significant uncertainties about diagnosis and prognosis in both PVS and MCS. These have increased rather than decreased in the last 20 years and this is why continued court oversight is necessary'.*

Legislative attempts to liberalise the law on assisted suicide

Since 2003, there have been over ten attempts to introduce assisted suicide across the parliaments of the United Kingdom. All of them have been rejected.

Coroners and Justice Bill (2009)

During the passage of what became the Coroners and Justice Act 2009, Lord Falconer proposed changing the law so that people would not be prosecuted for helping relatives travel to overseas suicide facilities to die. The proposal was defeated.

Assisted Dying for the Terminally Ill Bill (2003–2006)

Lord Joffe introduced Bills in the House of Lords unsuccessfully in 2003, 2004 and 2005. The Bills were similar in aim, seeking to legalise assisted suicide. The first Bill ran out of parliamentary time. The second Bill, entitled the 'Assisted Dying for the Terminally Ill Bill' and would have legalised assisted suicide for people who could not kill themselves. According to some commentators this would have come to the 'very brink of euthanasia'. Major concerns about public safety issues led to the failure of the Bill. Lord Joffe introduced his third Bill with the same title late in 2005. This was defeated by a majority of 148–100 at Second Reading in May 2006.

The Lords Select Committee on Medical Ethics (1992–1994)

In 1992 a Select Committee of the House of Lords was established to consider the ethical, legal and clinical implications of life-shortening actions. The report in 1994 rejected any proposal to: 'cross the line which prohibits any intentional killing, a line which we think it essential to preserve'. The Report also rejected any change in the law on assisted suicide. The Government accepted this recommendation.

End of Life Assistance Bill (Scotland) (2010–2012)

Independent MSP Margo MacDonald tabled Bills in 2010 and 2011 that would have legalised assisted suicide. Under the second Bill people born with disabilities who 'lose the will to live' would have been eligible to end their lives. The first Bill was defeated by the Scottish Parliament and the second Bill was rejected at public consultation phase.

Lord Falconer Bill (2014)

Having suffered a heavy defeat in the previous parliamentary session, Lord Falconer continued his efforts to change the law, establishing a so-called independent Commission on Assisted Dying in November 2010. However, the independence of the Commission was called into question. Nine of the twelve members appointed by Lord Falconer were known to favour a change in the law prior to their appointment; the remaining Commissioners were not known to oppose assisted suicide. Supported by Dignity in Dying, the leading UK pressure group campaigning for assisted suicide, and funded by the late Sir Terry Pratchett (a known advocate of assisted suicide), more than 40 organisations chose not to give evidence to the Commission including the British Medical Association and a number of Christian organisations.

Following the publication of the Commission report, in May 2013, Lord Falconer introduced a Bill in the House of Lords seeking to legalise assisted suicide in England and Wales. Owing to the constraints of the parliamentary timetable, there was no time for a Second Reading (debate on the general principles of the Bill) in the House of Lords before the end of the parliamentary session.

Proponents of assisted suicide ensured that, in the space of four months from December 2013 – March 2014, the House of Lords debated assisted suicide on three separate occasions. None of the debates resulted in a vote (nor could they have done).

Lord Falconer introduced a second Bill – the 'Assisted Dying Bill' – to the House of Lords in June 2014 when it received its First Reading. As before, the Bill sought to make it legal for a terminally ill, mentally competent adult with less than six months to live to be helped to kill themselves in England and Wales. The Bill was given a Second Reading (at which point there is a general debate on the principles of the Bill) on 18 July 2014 where it was subject to ten hours of rigorous debate with roughly equal numbers of Peers speaking for and against. As is commonplace with Private Members' Bills, the Assisted Dying Bill automatically passed its Second Reading with no need for a vote. The Committee Stage, involving line-by-line examination of the Bill took place on 7 November 2014 and 16 January 2015.

At Committee Stage more than 175 amendments were tabled to the Bill – largely from Peers opposed to assisted suicide. Such an unusually large number of amendments

meant that it was unlikely – given the constraints of the parliamentary timetable – that the Bill would progress any further.

Of note, on the first day of Committee, 7 November, an amendment was made to the Bill which called for judges, rather than doctors, to be the arbiters of whether someone should be allowed access to assisted suicide. Although votes on amendments can and do take place at Committee Stage, it is the convention in the House of Lords that Committee Stage should be exploratory, with voting more properly belonging to Report Stage. Proponents of assisted suicide went against this convention in pushing through the amendment. On the second day of Committee on 16 January, two amendments which would have tightened the scope of the Bill were rejected.

Although euthanasia and assisted suicide are not devolved matters, in December 2014 the Welsh Assembly debated a motion in support of the principles of Lord Falconer's Assisted Dying Bill. Happily, AMs voted by 21 votes to 12 against the motion and therefore even the principles of the Bill (there were also 20 abstentions). That one of the jurisdictions to which Lord Falconer's Bill would have applied rejected the mere principles of the Bill was very encouraging.

Following the dissolution of Parliament on 30 March, the Lord Falconer's Bill fell.

Rob Marris Assisted Dying Bill (2015)

The MP Rob Marris based this Bill on the Falconer Bill. It was defeated in its Second Reading in 2015 following a lengthy debate. The Bill was defeated by 330 to 118.

Euthanasia and assisted dying rates are soaring. But where are they legal?

It is available in a growing number of countries and jurisdictions – but not the UK, where it remains outlawed.

By Nicola Davis

What's the difference between euthanasia, assisted dying and assisted suicide?

'The main difference between euthanasia and assisted suicide is who performs the final, fatal act,' said Richard Huxtable, professor of medical ethics and law at the University of Bristol.

Euthanasia refers to active steps taken to end someone's life to stop their suffering and the 'final deed' is undertaken by someone other than the individual, for example a doctor. If the person concerned has requested this, it falls under the term 'voluntary euthanasia'.

Assisted suicide is about helping someone to take their own life at their request – in other words the final deed is undertaken by the person themselves. Assisted dying can be used to mean both euthanasia, generally voluntary, and assisted suicide; however, some campaign groups use it to refer only to assisted suicide of terminally ill people.

'One of the dilemmas we have in these ongoing debates is how people use the various phrases,' says Huxtable. Most, but not all, jurisdictions that allow some form of euthanasia or assisted suicide require the involvement of medical professionals.

Palliative sedation, in which people can request to be kept under deep sedation until they die, is allowed in many countries, including the Netherlands and France – is not euthanasia.

Which countries permit any of these variants?

The Netherlands and Switzerland are the most well known, and Belgium considered perhaps the most liberal, but several other jurisdictions allow some form of euthanasia or assisted suicide. That said, permitted circumstances differ considerably.

In the Netherlands both euthanasia and assisted suicide are legal if the patient is enduring unbearable suffering and there is no prospect of improvement. Anyone from the age of 12 can request this, but parental consent is required if a child is under 16. There are a number of checks and balances, including that doctors must consult with at least one other, independent doctor on whether patient meets the necessary criteria.

Belgium, Luxembourg, Canada and Colombia also allow both euthanasia and assisted suicide, although there are differences – for example only terminal patients can request it in Colombia, while Belgium has no age restriction for children (although they must have a terminal illness).

Assisted suicide is more widely available than euthanasia. Among the places where people can choose to end their life this way are Switzerland and a number of US states including California, Colorado, Hawaii, New Jersey, Oregon, Washington state, Vermont and the District of Columbia. Laws permitting assisted suicide came into force in the Australian state of Victoria last month.

Again, the exact circumstances in which assisted suicide is allowed vary, with some jurisdictions – Oregon and Vermont – only allowing it in the case of terminal illness. For some places it is permitted not because laws have been passed, but because laws do not prohibit it. For example in Switzerland it is an offence to assist a suicide if it is done with selfish motives. 'The result of that is there is this growth of not-for-profit organisations,' says Prof. Penney Lewis, an expert on the law around end-of-life care at King's College London.

Other countries, including New Zealand, are considering legalising some form of euthanasia.

What's the situation in the UK?

Euthanasia and assisted suicide are illegal. Euthanasia can lead to a murder charge and assisted suicide could result in a sentence of up to 14 years in prison.

A royal precedent

Euthanasia is illegal in the UK – but in 1936 it seems there was at least one patient whose doctor decided to actively end his suffering: King George V.

The king's health had been declining and by early 1936 it was clear the end was near – on 20 January his chief physician, Lord Dawson, announced that death was imminent. The king died shortly before midnight.

But decades later, when Dawson's personal notes were revealed by his biographer Francis Watson, it emerged that this end was engineered: Dawson admitted to giving the king a lethal mix of morphine and cocaine to hasten his death.

'Hours of waiting just for the mechanical end when all that is really life has departed only exhausts the onlookers and keeps them so strained that they cannot avail themselves of the solace of thought, communion or prayer. I therefore decided to determine the end,' he wrote.

However, he also added that his actions meant news of the king's death could be broken in the morning edition of *The Times*.

That said, anonymous surveys suggest euthanasia does occur in the UK – but it is very rare. A study published in 2009 using responses from more than 3,700 medical professionals suggested 0.2% of deaths involve voluntary euthanasia and 0.3% involved euthanasia without explicit patient request – no assisted suicide was recorded.

It is not normally illegal for a patient to be given treatment to relieve distress that could indirectly shorten life – but this is not euthanasia. It is already legal in the UK for patients to refuse treatment, even if that could shorten their life, and for medical care to be withdrawn by doctors in certain cases, for example where a patient is in a vegetative state and will not recover (sometimes controversially called passive euthanasia).

How many people undergo euthanasia or assisted suicide?

Total figures from around the world are hard to collate. Figures from Switzerland show that the numbers of those living in the country who underwent assisted suicide rose from 187 in 2003 to 965 in 2015.

According to the 2017 Regional Euthanasia Review Committees (RTE), in the Netherlands there were 6,585 cases of voluntary euthanasia or assisted suicide – 4.4% of the total number of deaths. About 96% of cases involved euthanasia, with less than 4% assisted suicide, and the largest proportion of cases involved people with cancer.

Agnes van der Heide, professor of decision-making and care at the end of life at the Erasmus University Medical Center in Rotterdam, says the reason euthanasia is more common than assisted suicide in the Netherlands is multifaceted. Doctors may feel that by performing the deed themselves they can have more control over dosages and the time the procedure takes.

'Patients are often in a very advanced stage of their disease where it is practically difficult if not impossible to drink the lethal drink they have to take when they chose for assistance in suicide,' she adds. 'It is a very bitter-tasting drink and it is quite an effort to drink it until the end,' she added. There might also be an element of viewing the act as a medical procedure and hence preferring a physician to do the job.

Lewis says the vast majority of people do not end their lives by euthanasia even if they can. 'There is far more withdrawal of life-sustaining treatment, even in jurisdictions that permit euthanasia,' she says.

What happened in the case of the Dutch teenager Noa Pothoven?

Noa Pothoven, who was 17, died last month – she had anorexia and severe depression. At first media reports suggested she had been 'legally euthanised', but later reports said it was unclear how she died, with her friends releasing a comment saying that she died after she stopped eating and drinking.

Van der Heide said that while she could not comment on Pothoven's case, it is possible for minors over the age of 12 to seek euthanasia or assisted suicide in the Netherlands, under certain conditions.

Has there been suicide tourism?

In some places, yes. According to van der Heide, while suicide tourism is not formally forbidden in the Netherlands, physicians must work with the patient to establish that they meet certain criteria. 'I think if a physician would provide euthanasia to a patient he doesn't know then it is very likely that the regional committee would have a problem with that,' she says.

However, people do travel to Switzerland for assisted suicide. According to statistics from Dignitas, 221 people travelled to the country for this purpose in 2018, 87 of whom were from Germany, 31 from France and 24 from the UK.

Legalisation state of euthanasia and physician-assisted suicide in selected countries

Country	Euthanasia	Physician-assisted Suicide	Age requirement	Required diagnosis	Symptom state
Switzerland	Illegal	Legal*	none specified	None	none
Netherlands	Legal	Legal	12	None	Unbearable suffering with no prospect of improvement
Luxembourg	Legal	Legal	18	None	Incurable condition with constant unbearable suffering and no prospect of improvement
Colombia	Legal	Legal	6	Terminal phase	terminal phase of a disease
Canada	Legal	Legal	18	None	Grievous and irremediable medical condition with enduring and unbearable suffering
Belgium	Legal	Legal	none	None adults, terminal children	Medically futile condition with unbearable mental or physical suffering

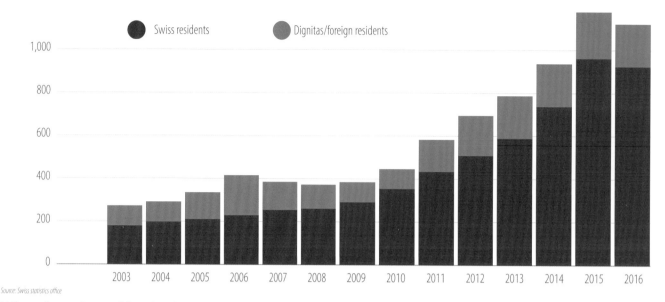

The number of assisted suicides in Switzerland has risen more than fourfold in little more than a decade

● Swiss residents   ● Dignitas/foreign residents

Source: Swiss statistics office

What does the public think about euthanasia and assisted suicide?

It depends a bit on the question you ask. A recent poll conducted by the National Centre for Social Research for MDMD found that 93% of people in the UK approved of, or wouldn't rule out, doctor-assisted suicide if the person is terminally ill.

The British Social Attitudes survey, published in 2017, sheds light on views about voluntary euthanasia, showing that people generally support the idea of doctors ending the life of a terminally ill person who requests it (78%), but that there is less support for a close relative doing the job (39%). It also shows that fervent support for voluntary euthanasia was lower if the person in question has a non-terminal illness or is dependent on relatives for all their needs but not terminal or in pain.

What do doctors think?

Euthanasia and assisted suicide have proved contentious among doctors. Some argue that support for such ideas goes against the commitment to 'do no harm'. Others say some people might choose not to end their life if they are made aware that they could be made comfortable with good end-of-life care.

'Some health professionals are familiar with the care of dying patients and with what palliative care can do – so they may have a feeling that assisted dying isn't always necessary,' says Dominic Wilkinson, professor of medical ethics at the University of Oxford.

But some doctors are supportive – at least for particular circumstances such as terminal illness – saying it can be a humane act, and that individuals should be allowed autonomy in when to die. After many years of opposing assisted dying, this year the Royal College of Physicians shifted its stance to become neutral on the subject following a poll of 7,000 UK hospital doctors in which 43.4% opposed allowing assisted dying and 31.6% supported it. The Royal College of GPs has recently announced it is going to start a consultation with members for their views.

The Debbie Purdy case

In the UK there have been a number of legal cases brought in an attempt to change the law around assisted suicide, including those by Tony Nicklinson, who had locked-in syndrome, and Diane Pretty, who had motor neurone disease. While these became high profile, they did not succeed.

However, the case brought by Debbie Purdy was different. Purdy, who had multiple sclerosis, sought clarification through the courts on what would happen to her husband if he were to help her to travel to Switzerland where she could access assisted suicide. Under UK law, such an act could be punishable by up to 14 years in prison.

Purdy was partially successful – and in 2010 the then director of public prosecutions, Kier Starmer, issued guidelines which set out factors that should be considered regarding whether someone should be prosecuted for helping another to take their own life – such as their motivations, and whether the police were informed.

'It turns out that you are extremely unlikely to be prosecuted for, for example, taking your loved one to Switzerland so they can have an assisted death,' says Penney Lewis. But she says that is no guarantee, and there could still be an investigation. 'There are plenty of stories of people describing unpleasant experiences with the police, many of which last months,' she adds.

Richard Huxtable agrees. '[The CPS guidance] is not giving a blueprint for how you might lawfully perform assistance in suicide,' he says.

In the Netherlands, a survey of almost 1,500 physicians published in 2015 found more than 90% of GPs and 87% of elderly care physicians supported the liberal Dutch approach to euthanasia and assisted suicide. That might be because the development of the laws was carried out with input from the medical profession.

'All the criteria and also the practice of euthanasia is mainly shaped by how physicians feel it should be,' says van der Heide. 'I think for the typical patient with end-stage cancer and severe unbearable suffering, there is hardly any physician in the Netherlands who thinks that the issue of harming patients is at stake there.'

Have the laws been a success?

That depends how you look at it. Support for the Dutch laws clearly remains high, but some say there are signs of a 'slippery slope', with the practice being applied too widely.

As van der Heide points out, the Dutch laws were designed with cases like terminal cancer in mind – but while cancer patients still make up the majority of requests, the proportion of requests related to other conditions is growing. 'Gradually of course [it] became more known to both physicians and patients what the requirements were and that they could also apply to other categories,' she says.

That has led to controversy. The 2017 RTE report recorded concerns by Dutch psychiatrists and doctors about the use of euthanasia for people with psychiatric disorders and patients in a very advanced stage of dementia. The 2015 survey found of the almost 1,500 responses that 31% of GPs and 25% of elderly care physicians would grant assisted dying for patients with advanced dementia, with the figures at 37% and 43% respectively for those with psychiatric problems.

However, as Huxtable points out, other jurisdictions including Oregon show that broadening of use is not inevitable. 'The fact there has been some slide in the Netherlands should give everyone reason to pause,' he says. 'We should think right from the outset what do we think in principle is defensible and are we going to – and we should – police the boundaries.'

There have also been allegations of malpractice. In 2018 both the Netherlands and Belgium reported their first cases in which doctors were investigated for possibly breaching the laws, with three more investigations under way in the Netherlands involving the euthanasia of psychiatric patients.

'Nowadays there are more controversial cases, so the likelihood that there now will be cases that do not fulfil the criteria to the extent that the public prosecutor thinks it is necessary to install a criminal procedure is more likely than it used to be,' says van der Heide.

Are there other concerns?

There have been concerns by disabilities groups that as euthanasia and assisted suicide become more common, it could put a pressure on those living with non-terminal conditions to end their lives. But van der Heide says doctors in the Netherlands take great care when dealing with requests to make sure patients meet strict requirements, and turn down those who do not.

She adds that the development of laws to allow euthanasia or assisted dying must be handled carefully. 'I indeed acknowledge that having a system in which euthanasia is an option should be really carefully monitored and researched because it in principle involves the risk of life of vulnerable people being regarded as less worthy or more prone to doctors' assistance in dying,' she says.

15 July 2019

Dutch authorities have recorded a threefold rise in euthanasia and assisted suicide since 2002

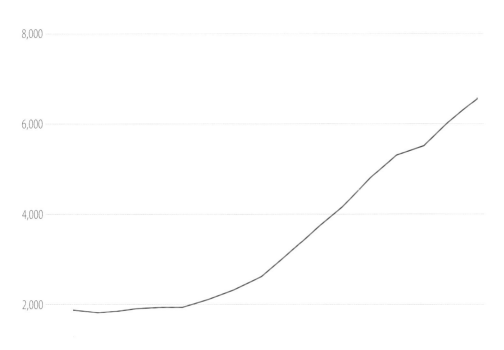

Source: Dutch regional euthanasia review committees

Countries where euthanasia is legal

Assisted dying is allowed in a growing number of countries – but not the UK.

By James Ashford

Euthanasia is illegal under English law, but the number of countries where it is permitted is growing.

Those in favour say that in a civilised society, people should be able to choose when they are ready to die and should be helped if they are unable to end their lives on their own.

But some critics take a moral stance against euthanasia and assisted suicide, saying life is given by God and only God can take it, says the BBC. Others think that laws allowing euthanasia could be abused and people who didn't want to die could be killed.

The terminology around euthanasia is sometimes inconsistently applied, but there is a difference between euthanasia, assisted suicide and assisted dying, says *The Guardian*.

Euthanasia refers to an instance where active steps are taken to end someone's life, but the fatal act is carried out by someone else, such as a doctor.

Assisted suicide is when someone takes their own life but is assisted by somebody else. Rather than a doctor carrying out the fatal act, they themselves do so.

Assisted dying can refer to either euthanasia or assisted suicide.

Under the Suicide Act 1961, both euthanasia and assisted suicide are criminal offences in the UK. Euthanasia can result in a murder charge, and assisted suicide by aiding or even counselling somebody in relation to taking their own life is punishable by 14 years' imprisonment.

But there are countries where euthanasia is legal, usually under strict conditions.

Switzerland

Probably the first country that comes to mind in relation to assisted dying, Switzerland allows physician-assisted suicide without a minimum age requirement, diagnosis or symptom state.

However, assisted suicide is deemed illegal if the motivations are 'selfish' – for example, if someone assisting the death stands to inherit earlier, or if they don't want the burden of caring for a sick person.

Euthanasia is not legal in the country.

In 2018, 221 people travelled to the Swiss clinic Dignitas for assisted suicide. Of these, 87 were from Germany, 31 from France and 24 from the UK.

About 1.5% of Swiss deaths are the result of assisted suicide.

Netherlands

Euthanasia and assisted suicide are legal in the Netherlands in cases where someone is experiencing unbearable suffering and there is no chance of it improving. There is no requirement to be terminally ill, and no mandatory waiting period.

Children as young as 12 can request assisted dying, but parental consent is needed for those under 16.

There are various checks that have to be undertaken before assisted dying can be approved. Doctors who are considering allowing assisted dying must consult with at least one other, independent doctor to confirm that the patient meets the necessary criteria.

Belgium

Belgium allows euthanasia and assisted suicide for those with unbearable suffering and no prospect of improvement. If a patient is not terminally ill, there is a one-month waiting period before euthanasia can be performed.

Belgium has no age restriction for children, but they must have a terminal illness to meet the criteria for approval.

Luxembourg

Assisted suicide and euthanasia are both legal in Luxembourg for adults. Patients must have an incurable condition with constant, intolerable suffering and no prospect of improvement.

Canada

Canada allows euthanasia and assisted suicide for adults suffering from 'grievous and irremediable conditions' whose death is 'reasonably foreseeable'.

In Quebec, only euthanasia is allowed.

Colombia

Terminal patients can request voluntary euthanasia in Colombia, and the first such death happened in 2015. An independent committee must approve the request for assisted dying.

Australia

The Australian state of Victoria passed voluntary euthanasia laws in November 2017 after 20 years and 50 failed attempts. The Australian Senate had previously repealed the law in 1997 owing to a public backlash against the 1995 law that allowed it.

To qualify for legal approval, you have to be an adult with decision-making capacity, you must be a resident of Victoria, and have intolerable suffering due to an illness that gives you a life expectancy of less than six months, or 12 months if suffering from a neurodegenerative illness.

And a doctor cannot bring up the idea of assisted dying, the patient must raise it first.

You have to make three requests to the scheme, including one in writing. You must then be assessed by two experienced doctors, one of whom is a specialist, to determine your eligibility, says The Guardian.

If eligible, you will be prescribed drugs which you must keep in a 'locked box' until a time of your choosing. If you can't administer the fatal drugs yourself, a doctor can administer a lethal injection.

USA

Several states now offer legal assisted dying. Oregon, Washington, Vermont, California, Colorado, Washington

DC, Hawaii, New Jersey, Maine and Montana all have laws or court rulings allowing doctor-assisted suicide for terminally ill patients.

Doctors can write patients a prescription for the fatal drugs, but a healthcare professional must be present when they are administered.

All of the states require a 15-day waiting period between two oral requests and a two-day waiting period between a final written request and the fulfilling of the prescription.

France

Palliative sedation, in which someone can ask to be deeply sedated until they die, is permitted in France, but assisted dying is not.

New Zealand

A Bill legalising voluntary euthanasia passed its second vote in parliament in June by 70 votes to 50, says the NZ Herald.

However, a third and final reading is still required before the Bill is passed into law, and it is far from guaranteed that it will succeed.

For now, both euthanasia and assisted suicide remain illegal.

28 August 2019

Assisted dying: does the law need to change?

By John Humphrys

If you were suffering a terminal illness, with only a limited time left to live, and with the certain prospect of your suffering cruelly increasing before your death finally releases you, should you be able to seek help to die sooner? It is a question that seems to face increasing numbers of people, struck down by incurable illnesses that kill only slowly and it is one that has bedevilled our society for many years now. But those who ask it come up against the same stern answer. No, you cannot seek such help because the law forbids it. Is the law right to do so?

Harrowing stories of people facing such unimaginably cruel ends to their lives seem to be becoming ever more frequent. And each time they reach the headlines they attract strong responses both from those who think the law is helping to perpetuate unnecessary suffering and from those who fear that changing the law could have consequences that might cause even more suffering.

This week yet another case brought the issue once again to the fore.

Geoff Whaley, an 80-year-old retired chartered accountant from Buckinghamshire, was diagnosed two years ago with Motor Neurone Disease, an affliction he knew would gradually deprive him of the use of every part of his body, and which is incurable. He decided that ultimately he would take himself to the Dignitas clinic in Switzerland. If doctors there satisfied themselves that his illness was terminal, that he did not have long to live and, most importantly, that he was taking the decision to end his life prematurely of his own free will, they would provide him with a lethal drink which he would administer to himself. He would then be dead within the hour.

In December, Mr Whaley was told by his doctors that he had between six and nine months left. So he decided that while he still had the physical capacity to pick up the lethal drink and to swallow it, he should make his way to Zurich without delay. He asked Ann, his wife, to make the necessary travel arrangements as he was no longer capable of physically doing so himself.

The Whaleys had made no secret of their intentions among their family and friends, from whom they received much support. But after an anonymous tip-off to the social services, the police became involved. It became immediately apparent to the officers who visited him at home that Mr Whaley was wholly mentally competent to take the decision and that he was doing so on what he regarded as rational grounds. Suicide is not a criminal offence so the police had no need to take further action with regard to him. But they then interviewed Ann Whaley, twice under caution. Under Section Two of the 1961 Suicide Act it is an offence to assist anyone in committing suicide, with a penalty of up to fourteen years in prison for anyone convicted of doing so. Was Mrs Whaley guilty of such an offence?

Mr Whaley told the BBC's home affairs editor, Mark Easton, that until this point he had been dealing with the planning of his own death in a wholly calm and controlled manner, but that after the police intervention 'I became completely terrified that control was going to be taken away from me. It shook me to the core.' He feared that his passport might be taken away, depriving him of the opportunity to travel to Switzerland. And of course he feared for the possible consequences for his wife.

She said that it was the first time in fifty-two years of marriage that she had seen him cry. But she had no doubt that she was right to be helping him in carrying out his plan to end his life early. She said: 'When you have a husband as brave as mine, you have to support him.'

The Whaleys travelled to Zurich days later and Geoff Whaley took his life on Thursday morning. Ann Whaley came back to England to face her grief and to the fear of what might happen to her. Although the police have said they do not intend to press charges against her, the case remains open and if new information comes to light, they may need to review the decision.

The Whaley case has not reached the courts and may never do so. The Crown Prosecution Service issued guidance some time ago saying that where it is clear that someone implicated in assisting a suicide has been 'wholly motivated by compassion' and that the person committing suicide took a 'voluntary, clear, settled and informed decision' to do so, then placing charges is unlikely. But some who have faced the same predicament as the Whaleys have actually chosen to seek help from the courts. Each time, as with the most recent case of Tony Nicklinson, another sufferer from Motor Neurone Disease, the courts, including the Supreme Court, have adopted an immensely sympathetic manner but responded that the law is the law and that they are in no position to override it.

That's why many people argue that the suffering of many terminally-dying people, such as Geoff Whaley and Tony Nicklinson – and the suffering of those who want to help them – can be allayed only by a change in the law.

Advocates of change have, at least for the moment, limited ambitions. They wish to change the law only in respect of people who are both terminally ill and still mentally capable of taking the decision to end their own lives. If a judge rules that both conditions are satisfied, then it should be lawful (they argue) for such a patient to seek help in ending their life prematurely and for the person providing that help to be able to do so lawfully. Mrs Whaley would then have been able to book flights to Zurich without fearing she was breaking the law.

But opponents of such a change in the law make several objections. In the first place, they say, it would expose those wondering whether or not to end their lives prematurely to emotional pressure, even from their families. They say the apparent safeguard that someone in this position would have to demonstrate they were of sound mind would be inadequate, since someone wholly in command of their mental faculties can still be susceptible to emotional pressure. Such a person might be in two minds about whether to end their own life but feel they ought to do so 'to save their families'. Only keeping the law as it can guard against such pressure, real or imagined.

The second objection is that legally allowing a third party to help someone to kill themselves will in many cases mean a doctor being the third party. This possibility has divided doctors themselves. Those doctors who support a change in the law argue that it is their job to relieve suffering and that to help someone suffering from a terminal illness by assisting them in dying early is precisely the relieving of suffering. But other doctors equally strongly believe that such a change in the law would radically alter the relationship between doctor and patient. In swearing the Hippocratic Oath, they argue, doctors commit themselves primarily to 'doing no harm', so deliberately ending a patient's life is utterly inconsistent with what a doctor is supposed to do, they argue.

The Royal College of Physicians is split down the middle on this question. A vote taken in 2014 established the college's opposition to doctors' involvement in assisted dying, but another vote is to be taken soon. The very fact that the decision is to be revisited so quickly after the last vote alarms doctors who continue to oppose a change in the law.

The third objection is that although the sort of change proposed now may be limited, it may turn out to be a 'slippery slope'. Opponents of the change fear that it could well lead to legalised euthanasia, a much broader licence to help people to die that some campaigners do indeed advocate.

It was these arguments which caused the Assisted Dying Bill to be thrown out by parliament when it was debated in 2015. Its advocate, the former Labour Lord Chancellor, Lord Falconer, continues to argue that the law will have to change. Of the Whaley case he said that it was 'monstrous' for Ann Whaley to be put in the position she found herself and described the existing law quite simply as a 'total pig'.

Is he right? Should we change the law so that the likes of Geoff Whaley, Tony Nicklinson and many others to come, can seek help from others when they want to die? Or is it too risky a move?

What's your view?

8 February 2019

Assisted dying: will the UK ever alter the law?

Yesterday's Supreme Court decision suggests not.

By Emma Diack

Yesterday the Supreme Court published its decision to reject the granting of permission for Noel Conway to bring his case to the Supreme Court. Another nail has been hammered into the coffin on altering the UK's law on assisted dying. The three justices (Lady Hale, Lord Reed and Lord Kerr) stated that 'not without some reluctance, it has been concluded that in this case those prospects are not sufficient to justify giving permission to appeal'.

Conway is a sufferer of motor neurone disease, a neurological condition which attacks the nerve cells responsible for controlling voluntary muscle movement. He was diagnosed in 2014 and is now in a wheelchair and possesses very little ability of movement below his neck. Dependent on a ventilator almost permanently, his muscles continue to degenerate and he finds it increasingly difficult to breathe. The former lecturer's case concerned the UK's laws on assisted suicide and how it should be legalised in certain circumstances.

The UK currently holds under section 2 of the Suicide Act 1961, that a person will be committing an offence if they 'encourage or assist the suicide or attempted suicide of another person'. So, while suicide itself is no longer a criminal offence, the input of others will be prosecuted. This subject has been, for years, up for considerable debate.

Advocates of legalising assisted dying often invoke arguments of allowing anyone who is suffering from a terminal illness should be given the right to decide how they may die. They should be given the opportunity to decide how and when they will die. For many individuals suffering from such illnesses they are often unable to commit the act of suicide themselves, and require the assistance of perhaps their partner or loved ones. As the current law stands, the patients loved ones may be prosecuted. This can include for example, aiding them to travel to Switzerland or another jurisdiction where assisted suicide is legal.

Prior to the Conway litigation, it was accepted 'that any right to die is contained within the right to respect for private and family life contained in Article 8' of the European Convention on Human Rights. Yet, each previous decision has been unsuccessful due to the establishment that 'any interference with that right is necessary in a democratic society for the purpose of preventing crime and protecting the rights of others'. Courts have been hesitant to declare the law incompatible because it believes it could harm the

vulnerable. This was reiterated in Nicklinson v Ministry of Justice where the Supreme Court asserted that parliament was the correct body to legislate on this issue.

Conway pursued a line of cases disputing this law. He sought to be allowed help to die when he has less than six months to live and still has the mental capacity to make the 'voluntary, clear, settled and informed' decision. He currently holds the common law right to end his own life by refusing consent to the continuation of his non-invasive ventilation (NIV) which helps him breathe.

However, he was concerned that he does not know how he will feel if his NIV is withdrawn and wanted to die in a dignified manner at a time of his own choosing. In July 2017, Conway and his legal team sought judicial review of the current law and 'a declaration of incompatibility with his rights under the ECHR' and proposed that 'assisted dying should be available to people aged 18 and above, who were of sound mind, with fewer than six months to live, and that each application should be reviewed by a High Court judge'.

In October 2017, this application was rejected by the High Court and then in January 2018 his challenge of that decision was rejected by the Court of Appeal. The decision by the Supreme Court to not hear his case in full means that it cannot proceed any further, and his efforts of altering the law on assisted suicide are lost.

Assisted suicide is a topic which emotes various ethical and moral dilemmas. Other jurisdictions such as the Netherlands and Switzerland have legalised euthanasia and assisted suicide. The State of Oregon has also legalised assisted suicide under their Death with Dignity Act in 1997. Why

should the UK not legislate on this issue? Is it not the right of a terminally ill patient to autonomously decide when to die? As Baroness Blackstone contended in the House of Lords reading of the 2014 Assisted Dying Bill:

'If we respect human rights, we should not deny those who know that they are dying the right to bring their lives to a more rapid end to alleviate their misery.'

It is likely that Conway will now turn to petition for parliament to alter the law, as it appears that the courts have provided no solace on this issue. However, the likelihood of parliament legislating on this issue is a slim one. In 2014, Lord Falconer attempted to pass the Assisted Dying Bill – this was rejected. The Bill was resubmitted and again rejected in 2017. Opponents of the Bill indicated reasons such as violating the sanctity of human life, that it places undue pressure on those believed to be vulnerable and that it could lead to a high proportion of terminally ill patients requesting death. It is a highly contentious issue.

Prior to Conway, it had been four years since the Supreme Court had heard a case on this issue, since Nicklinson. Perhaps not enough time had passed in order for the justices to come to a different conclusion. So, given case law history and rejected legislation on this issue, it is unlikely that the law will change any time soon.

28 November 2018

Assisted dying and the law; why you can be disinherited for helping a loved one to die

By Sarah Young, Partner and Samantha Hirst, Associate Solicitor of Ridley & Hall Legal Ltd

A court case earlier this year has highlighted an astonishingly cruel quirk of the law, where a wife who helped her terminally ill husband commit suicide in Switzerland, faced criminal prosecution as well as being disinherited on her return to the UK.

Assisted dying is illegal in the UK. It is legally available under various conditions in five European countries including Belgium and Switzerland, as well as in Canada and six US states.

Alexander Ninian who was 86 and terminally ill, went to Dignitas in Switzerland in 2017 to die, accompanied by his wife Sarah Ninian. Mr Ninian had a terminal condition, called progressive supra nuclear palsy. He obtained legal and medical advice beforehand and prepared a statement making it clear that his wife had been opposed to his decision and that he had made the decision of his own free will. Once Mr Ninian had made the necessary arrangements, his wife went with him to Dignitas because he was too disabled by his illness to travel alone. It was clear that theirs was a long and loving marriage and that Mr Ninian had a clear and unambiguous wish to die because of his condition.

Mrs Ninian was aware that she faced potential prosecution on her return to the UK under the Suicide Act 1961 for assisting her husband to commit suicide. The Crown Prosecution Service decided not to prosecute on the grounds that it would not be in the public interest to do so. But this was not the end of the matter, because the question then arose as to whether or not Mrs Ninian could inherit her husband's estate.

The Forfeiture Act 1982 lays down a simple rule that an individual cannot benefit from someone's death if they have 'unlawfully aided, abetted or procured' the death.

Mrs Ninian had to apply to the High Court to ask that the 'forfeiture rule' be waived in her case. The case (Ninian v Findlay) was decided in February 2019, following a hearing and the judge decided in her favour, so that she inherited her husband's estate in accordance with the terms of his will.

The case must have been hugely expensive and traumatic for the widow, at a time when she had just lost her much-loved husband.

Such a heavy handed approach by the law is surely anachronistic given that public attitudes towards suicide have changed considerably since the Suicide Act became law more than 50 years ago. To lose your spouse and then to find out that you may be barred from inheriting their estate – even if they have left a will in your favour – seems strikingly harsh.

On 4 July 2019 Parliament reviewed the law related to assisted suicide in a major commons debate. The review followed the case of Ann and Geoffrey Whaley, who were interviewed under police caution, after a tip-off to police that Geoffrey – who was suffering from motor neurone disease – was planning to travel to Switzerland to die at Dignitas. Ann Whaley has launched 'Acts of Love', a campaign that brings together families across the country who have been affected by the current law on assisted dying. This summer also, GPs were consulted on whether the Royal College of General Practitioners (RCGP) should change its position on assisted dying, which it currently opposes.

More generally, the law on assisted dying continues to impact very harshly on families; just last month the family of Mavis Eccleston spoke of their 'terrible ordeal' when their mother was cleared of murdering her husband of almost 60 years following a 'suicide pact' when both took an overdose of prescription drugs. Dennis Eccleston, 81, was terminally ill with cancer at the time and Mavis didn't want to live without him but survived the overdose when they were found by family members.

Although the issue of assisted dying is currently in the spotlight, there is no immediate sign that the law is going to change. In the meantime, surely if the CPS decides not to prosecute, the law should be changed so that the forfeiture rule does not apply in cases involving assisted dying.

16 October 2019

Article 2: Right to life

Article 2 protects your right to life

Article 2 of the Human Rights Act protects your right to life.

This means that nobody, including the Government, can try to end your life. It also means the Government should take appropriate measures to safeguard life by making laws to protect you and, in some circumstances, by taking steps to protect you if your life is at risk.

Public authorities should also consider your right to life when making decisions that might put you in danger or that affect your life expectancy.

If a member of your family dies in circumstances that involve the state, you may have the right to an investigation. The state is also required to investigate suspicious deaths and deaths in custody.

The courts have decided that the right to life does not include a right to die.

Separately, Protocol 13, Article 1 of the Human Rights Act makes the death penalty illegal in the UK.

Are there any restrictions to this right?

Article 2 is often referred to as an 'absolute right'. These are rights that can never be interfered with by the state. There are situations, however, when it does not apply.

For example, a person's right to life is not breached if they die when a public authority (such as the police) uses necessary force to:

- stop them carrying out unlawful violence
- make a lawful arrest
- stop them escaping lawful detainment, and
- stop a riot or uprising.

Of course, even in these circumstances, the force used must be essential and strictly proportionate. Force is 'proportionate' when it is appropriate and no more than necessary to address the problem concerned.

The positive obligation on the state to protect a person's life is not absolute. Due to limited resources, the state might not always be able to fulfil this obligation. This could mean, for example, that the state does not have to provide life-saving drugs to everyone in all circumstances.

Using this right – example

A social worker from the domestic violence team in a local authority used human rights arguments to get new accommodation for a woman and her family at risk of serious harm from a violent ex-partner. She based her case on the local authority's obligation to protect the family's right to life and the right not to be treated in an inhuman or degrading way.

(Example provided by the British Institute of Human Rights)

What the law says

Article 2: Right to life

1. Everyone's right to life shall be protected by law. No one shall be deprived of his life intentionally save in the execution of a sentence of a court following his conviction of a crime for which the penalty is provided by law.

2. Deprivation of life shall not be regarded as inflicted in contravention of this Article when it results from the use of force which is no more than absolutely necessary:

    - in defence of any person from unlawful violence
    - in order to effect a lawful arrest or to prevent the escape of a person lawfully detained, and
    - in action lawfully taken for the purpose of quelling a riot or insurrection.

Note: See Article 1 of Protocol 13 for the wording in the Act that makes the death penalty illegal in the UK.

Example case: Pretty v United Kingdom [2002]

A woman suffering from an incurable degenerative disease wanted to control when and how she died. To avoid an undignified death, she wanted her husband to help her take her life. She sought assurance that he would not be prosecuted, but the European Court of Human Rights found that the right to life does not create a right to choose death rather than life. It meant there was no right to die at the hands of a third person or with the assistance of a public authority.

Case summary taken from *Human rights, human lives: a guide to the Human Rights Act for public authorities*, which shares examples and legal case studies that show how human rights work in practice.

15 November 2018

www.equalityhumanrights.com

The debate on euthanasia and its legal progress around the world

By Matt Carter

Euthanasia is a practice that refers to an act that ends a person's life to prevent agony.

This practice, already recognised in Greek times, is now described as an action to cause the death of an individual suffering from an incurable disease. This one causes intolerable mental and/or physical suffering. Euthanasia is done by a specialised doctor or under the patient's own control.

Considering the fact that life expectancy has increased in industrialised countries followed by scientific and technological developments in the field of medicine, euthanasia is now a subject both very protected and sensitive.

Defining the term – not so simple

The acceleration of the end of life of a suffering person can be achieved by different means. These are not all being grouped under the term 'euthanasia' since the aim is not always the end of life itself.

Indeed, another practice, that of 'assisted suicide', provides an environment and means necessary for a person to carry out his or her own suicide, regardless of the motivations. It must be the patient himself who commits this act and not a third party. This applies even if it is a relative carrying this out.

This assistance requires a clear and free request from the applicant without any defects.

It is customary to separate active euthanasia, which refers to a voluntary act to shorten a patient's life, from the passive euthanasia, which consists of stopping curative treatment or stopping the use of instruments or products that keep a patient alive. In the latter case, no means are used to hasten patient's death.

There is a classification of euthanasia by type of consent:

◆ **Voluntary euthanasia:** When an individual has the mental and physical capacity to seek help to die and asks for it.

◆ **Non-voluntary euthanasia:** The individual no longer has the mental and physical capacity to seek help to die but has previously expressed such a willingness.

◆ **Non-voluntary euthanasia (meaning 2):** When an individual no longer has the mental or physical capacity to seek help to die or to oppose it and it is not known what his or her will would have been.

Legislation and judicial practices status of national legislation

Many countries around the world do not recognise or prohibit euthanasia and other forms of end-of-life assistance. However, some of them recognise an implicit and/or explicit tolerance to ensure that these practices take place in a regulated environment.

This is the case in Belgium and Netherlands, where euthanasia is recognised under extremely specific conditions. In Luxembourg, euthanasia and assisted suicide are now completely legal.

On the other hand, in Switzerland only assisted suicide is allowed under conditions. But in France, it is considered a premeditated murder or poisoning. This is the case, even though measures have been taken to stop therapeutic persecution since 2005.

In the United States, euthanasia is authorised only for terminally ill patients. In Canada meanwhile, euthanasia is in law a reprehensible act, but in practice, some cases have been tolerated. For instance, in 2008, a jury acquitted Stéphan Dufour, accused of helping his sick uncle to take his own life.

Cases related to euthanasia

According to the most publicised cases, two cases in France recorded in 2008 (Rémy Salvat, 24 and Chantal Sébire, 52) were not enough for the country to review its laws.

One of the most controversial cases is in Canada with Robert Latimer, who killed his 12-year-old daughter severely affected by cerebral palsy. As in France, such acts are considered murder and are punishable by 14 years in prison in the United Kingdom.

At the European level, the European Court of Human Rights has always been reticent about the debate on euthanasia. Indeed, considering Article 2 of the European Convention on Human Rights, which explicitly indicates a right to life, this court has difficulty passing a 'right to death' which is an idea it totally opposed.

Since the progress of medicine in the preservation and extension of life has been decisive, the question has arisen of the limits to be placed on 'life support' practices.

The public debate on this subject led the medical profession, philosophers and theologians to debate the subject of quality of life, and the rights of a human being to determine when this quality has deteriorated as long as it becomes acceptable and lawful to put an end to his agony and suffering. This ultimately led states to legislate under the name of bio-ethical laws.

However, some, such as Hippocrates, had a different conception of things and, in the Hippocratic Oath, doctors are forbidden to use all forms of assisted suicide: 'I will refrain from all evil and injustice. I will not give poison to anyone, if asked, nor will I take the initiative to make such a suggestion.'

Euthanasia and religion

Catholicism

Euthanasia is in direct opposition to the 6th Commandment: 'You shall not kill.'

Consequently, all forms of euthanasia are prohibited and this prohibition denounces a 'death culture' of Western societies for which 'a life is deprived of any value'.

Indeed, for Catholics, the depth of Man's supernatural vocation reveals the greatness and price of his human life. This still applies, even in its temporal phase. But palliative care are still accepted.

Protestantism

Unlike Catholicism, some currents of Protestantism support the idea that God is not exclusive in having the right to life.

Indeed, the divine life represents a dynamism that comes from love and the bond that humans have for each other.

Islam

In this religion, human being represents the creature that bears the divine imprint and represents his power on Earth.

Active euthanasia is therefore legally prohibited since it is seen as a murder. The only thing allowed is to let the person die naturally but passive euthanasia is not prohibited.

Buddhism

Suicide is not recommended since the suppression of life is considered as a negative act. Nevertheless, the conviction of euthanasia is not automatic.

But the 14th Dalaï Lama warned against active euthanasia, explaining that by trying to escape the suffering of this life, we could face the same suffering in a future life and in more difficult conditions.

Judaism

Active euthanasia is doomed since it is God who gives life and the one who destroys a life, it is as if he destroys the whole universe.

But the Jews nevertheless make a concession, they renounce hopeless medical acts, that is to say passive euthanasia.

Arguments for and against euthanasia

For the Legalisation

Concerning the side for the legalisation of euthanasia, they have a lot of arguments on their side. These include the end of suffering, avoiding the clandestinity of euthanasia, a feeling of social uselessness.

The individual liberty is one of the important points behind this first plan. This is because they say that the human being is the only rights holder of his own body.

Furthermore, there is a utilitarian conception of morality. A sacrifice of some for the benefit of the greatest number (legit to optimise resources to privilege patients whose lives can be saved).

For some, the disease is perceived as an unacceptable degradation for the patient, which represents a certain human dignity.

Indeed, for people with neuro-degenerative diseases, they would like to have the possibility of choosing to die. Ideally, this would happen before they have a permanent loss of autonomy. This would allow them to avoid being totally dependent on the help of others.

Against the legalisation

For doctors, euthanasia is an offensive practice. It is also a disrespect for the Hippocratic Oath they are forced to take before they can even practice their profession.

Some people believe that as pain and suffering progresses, euthanasia becomes unnecessary.

In some religions, any suicide can be seen as a personal tragedy and a failure for society.

Apart from the human side, there are also people who are reluctant to euthanise for fear of drift and slippage if it is legalised.

Indeed, there would be risks such as financial and moral pressure on patients.

But also, euthanasia could become an instrument of social domination with the pecuniary motive. It could come to be seen as an easier, cheaper and faster solution with, in return, neglected palliative care.

18 January 2019

Disabled people like me fear legal assisted suicide: it suggests that some lives are less worth living

Disabled people look to doctors to help us live, not to help us die, writes Jane Campbell.

Many terminally ill and disabled people oppose assisted suicide.

Not a single organisation of, or for, disabled people, or one representing people with long-term health conditions has campaigned for assisted suicide to be legalised.

We recognise that Section 2 of the Suicide Act 1961 provides essential protection for all suicidal people, including terminally ill and disabled people.

If you believe that terminal illness or disability is sufficient reason to desire suicide, what does it say about your perceptions of terminally ill and disabled people? Are we really so different from you?

'But it's not about you,' is the challenge we hear most frequently. Those seeking to change the law claim to do so only for patients deemed to be terminally ill, with strict criteria to be met before an assisted suicide can be considered.

Readers of *The BMJ* will recognise that the distinction between disability and terminal illness is a false one: for many disabled people, a chest infection is a terminal illness unless treated. The disabled person dependant on a ventilator is terminally ill if the ventilator is switched off. I am many years over my prognosis end date, along with countless others who have a progressive condition.

Proponents of a change in the law believe that a line can be drawn between terminal illness and disability, that a binary test can be devised to decide who can have an assisted suicide and who cannot. Thus it becomes a treatment option for some, but not for others.

But terminal illness and disability do not exist in a vacuum. We all have views about them. Often these views include widely held perceptions involving loss, decline, and fear of the future. It is hard to be positive as a disabled person, especially when the media is full of stories of abuse, neglect, cut-backs, and over stretched resources. Even when medical and social care are at their best, our fear of the future remains.

Given this context, it is unsurprising that some patients develop suicidal thoughts, which perhaps will be endorsed by family, friends, and members of the medical team. A

change in the law would thus permit the focus to switch from preserving life to ending life. It is harder to think of a more fundamental change in the doctor-patient relationship.

For disabled people this is profoundly worrying. We know that it can take years to adjust to illness and disability. A person's outlook can be revolutionised with the right health and social care, but this can take years to put in place and remains elusive to many. Would it be right to grant an assisted suicide to someone who feels that they are a 'bed blocker' and is tired of waiting for the right support?

We rely on the medical profession in our darkest hours. You seldom see us at our best. You often see us when we are in crisis. Yet we depend on you to do all that you can for us. Whether you admire us or pity us you do your utmost.

Many of us, myself included, are alive now because of the skill of the medical profession, advances in drug treatments, and improved devices. We are immensely grateful. We want you to keep asking yourselves, 'How can I improve this person's health and quality of life?' Now is not the time to give up on us to vote neutral on assisted suicide.

Not Dead Yet UK is a UK-based network that is part of a global alliance of disabled people who oppose euthanasia and assisted suicide.

Competing interests: *I have read and understood the BMJ Group policy on declaration of interests and declare the following interest: I am a severely disabled person whose life depends upon the care I currently receive from the NHS. I am fearful that any change to the current law prohibiting assisted suicide may adversely affect how I, other disabled friends and the wider community of disabled people are treated in the future, especially should they become less able to make my wishes known.*

Definitions under dispute

Proponents and opponents of assisted dying do not all agree on the terminology used to describe the process.

Assisted dying – Proponents of the Assisted Dying Bill 2015 in England and Wales argue that this term best describes prescribing life ending drugs for terminally ill, mentally competent adults to administer themselves after meeting strict legal safeguards. Assisted dying, as defined like this, is legal and regulated in the US states of Oregon, Vermont, Washington, Montana, Hawaii, California, and Colorado, and in Washington, DC. In 2017, similar legislation was passed in Victoria, Australia.

Assisted suicide – This term is often intended to describe giving assistance to die to people with long term progressive conditions and other people who are not dying, in addition to patients with a terminal illness. The drugs are self administered. Some opponents of assisted dying do not accept that it is different from assisted suicide. Assisted suicide, as defined like this, is permitted in Switzerland.

Voluntary euthanasia – This term describes a doctor directly administering life-ending drugs to a patient who has given consent. Voluntary euthanasia is permitted in the Netherlands, Belgium, and Luxembourg. In 2016, Canada legalised both voluntary euthanasia and assisted dying for people whose death is 'reasonably foreseeable,' in what it calls 'medical assistance in dying' (MAID).

6 February 2019

Tetraplegic model speaks out against euthanasia after once planning to end her life

As the End of Life Choice Bill is currently being debated in New Zealand, a woman, Claire Freeman, involved in a car accident causing her to become tetraplegic, has spoken out forcefully against the Bill.

The Bill permits assisted suicide in cases where an adult has a 'terminal illness that is likely to end the person's life within six months'; or suffers from 'a grievous and irremediable medical condition; and is in an advanced state of irreversible decline in capability; and experiences unbearable suffering that cannot be relieved in a manner that he or she the person considers tolerable'.

Claire argues that this Bill would have been dangerous for people like her given her (former) 'mind-set and lack of proper support' and had this Bill passed only a few years ago, she would have been eligible to end her life.

Although formerly pro-assisted suicide, her experience as a tetraplegic has led her to change her mind admitting that '[she] didn't really understand the implications of having a 'choice' [for assisted suicide]'.

Claire attempted suicide more than once and her health professionals 'encouraged [her] to explore assisted suicide'. She had intended to travel to Switzerland to kill herself but was unable to do so due to a disastrous operation on her neck, which made her condition even worse.

During her recuperation in hospital '[she] realised that being offered assisted suicide instead of suicide support was disturbing'.

'I had been told "if I was in your position, with your disability, I wouldn't want to live" by the very health professionals who are there to help suicide survivors. No one ever asked about my toxic mind-set and frantic way of living.

'I realised my biggest problem had been my mind-set and a lack of proper support'

Claire said that people like her are not being given a voice in this debate in New Zealand.

'I don't want to see a vulnerable person talking to a health professional who assumes their life is of little value due to their disability or illness.'

'The reality is this: if the End of Life Choice Bill, in its current form, were law four years ago, I'd be dead. This isn't about religion or politics; it's about trying to do the right thing and highlight the dangers of this bill.'

Clare McCarthy of Right To Life UK commented:

'The attitude of medical professionals towards people with disabilities in this case is, sadly, all too familiar. '

'These professionals acted in a remarkably unprofessional manner by encouraging Claire to kill herself, and, as she rightly notes, she would not be alive today had the law been different. We can see clearly that the attitudes of the medical professionals and the lack of proper support were a key motivating factor behind Claire's original decision to take her life, which, fortunately, she was unable to enact.

'As her experience shows, laws prohibiting assisted suicide and euthanasia protect people like Claire, and they should not be removed.'

7 June 2019

The risks of legalising assisted suicide are simply too great

By James Mildred

MPs will again debate assisted suicide today during a backbench business debate. The debate won't change the law and there won't be a vote, but it will provide an opportunity for the key arguments on both sides to be heard.

This is a very sensitive and challenging issue. The stories of intense suffering at the end of life provoke only sympathy and understanding. We fear a bad death and so we look to find ways of controlling the circumstances, so suffering is minimised, and people are empowered to make their own choices. But hard cases make bad laws and MPs need to balance the desires of a minority, with the pressures that would fall on thousands upon thousands of vulnerable people. The current law, which prohibits any form of assisted suicide or euthanasia is the safest way of doing so.

Time after time over the last decade, MPs and Peers have consistently rejected assisted suicide proposals. This is no accident. There are powerful reasons why resisting attempts to change the current law should remain the priority. Legalising assisted suicide would open Pandora's box and despite all the protestations from the other side, public safety would be put at risk.

But people feel very strongly that we can make a law that is safe, reasonable and allows certain people the option of assisted suicide. Well, the onus is on them to prove it, beyond reasonable doubt. It is no good naively saying that the 'safeguards' will work. Where is the proof? This matters intensely because the risks of failure in this regard are exceptionally high and involve people's lives.

Naturally, some will argue society and its attitudes towards this issue have fundamentally changed. They will point to polling which will show mass public support for a change in the law. But we all know polling can be misleading. Nor are policy makers obliged to follow polling when it comes to policy. That's not to say the views of the public don't matter, rather we must handle polling with care. In 2014, polling showed that when people were presented with the five key arguments against legalising assisted suicide, support dropped dramatically to below 50%. The point is that while large sections of the media seem to support a law change, this can lead to an inaccurate assessment of where most people are on this issue.

Since the last vote in 2015, where MPs rejected the Assisted Dying Bill by 330 to 118, the reality is nothing has changed when it comes to the dangers associated with legalising some form of assisted suicide. In fact, the evidence from other jurisdictions where assisted suicide is legal overwhelmingly tells us to go in a different direction.

If you look at what has happened in other jurisdictions, incremental expansion follows the introduction of assisted suicide laws. Both in Belgium and the Netherlands, the euthanasia laws have been expanded. In Belgium, euthanasia was legalised in 2002. Then in 2014, the law was amended to include children experiencing constant and unbearable suffering which cannot be eased, and which will cause death in the short term. People have been euthanised in Belgium due to depression, blindness, deafness, gender-identity crisis and anorexia.

In the Netherlands, meanwhile, there has been a steady increase in euthanasia deaths. In 2017, they accounted for four per cent of total Dutch deaths. There is evidence of a worrying trend of so called 'Romeo and Juliet' cases where couples are euthanised together.

Even if the examples of Belgium and the Netherlands are dismissed because what is being proposed here is a much narrower law, there is always Washington State, where 56% of those who died under the Death with Dignity Act said they were concerned with being a burden on family, friends or caregivers. In the state of Oregon, in 2018, more than half of those seeking assisted suicide, as a reason for doing so said they didn't want to be a burden on loved ones. Given the already existing tendency among older people to fear being a burden, the evidence from these States should make us stop and think.

Contrary to the misleading impression given by assisted suicide proponents, in Oregon there is also evidence of expansion, with more medical conditions now considered in the scope of the law when compared with 1998–99. They also recently changed the law so doctors could waive the 15-day waiting period which was included in the original legislation as a safeguard to protect vulnerable and depressed people who might change their minds.

What we need to grasp is that the introduction of assisted suicide would represent a profound and devastating change in society when it comes to how we view the value of life. If we legalise it for those with just six months left, what is to stop us overtime going even further? The classic argument for assisted suicide – that it is up to an individual and it should be their choice to do as they wish – fails to recognise that our choices have consequences.

4 July 2019

The slippery slope to death by doctor's order

The Royal College of Physicians' decision to end its opposition to assisted dying is morally indefensible and gives a green light to activists.

By Neil Scolding

Imagine (if you will) a progressive movement, a modernising trend, opposed by the majority, supported by an enlightened minority. Imagine (it won't be difficult) the radical minority to be full of passionate intensity, certain that their view must prevail. They call a vote. The electorate gets it wrong and rejects them. The electorate is instructed to vote again. They get it wrong again. Now what? You cannot stop the march of history! Obviously there must be a third election, but too much is being left to chance. So you make two innovative and imaginative changes. First, you don't so much shift as walk away with the goalposts; and second, announce the result in advance. So another vote is called, and simultaneously the outcome declared. Unless two-thirds oppose your change, the new, progressive position will now be adopted. Simple!

Now open your eyes.

This is precisely what has recently unfolded, not in some newly-assembled underground rabble of revolutionaries, but within one of the largest and most influential medical institutions in the world, the Royal College of Physicians of London. The 'progressive' issue in question is assisted dying, in particular the College's long-held stance of opposing legalisation. The RCP's third poll since 2006, complete with its novel approach to democracy, has been completed after a minor adjustment: the RCP Council initially decreed that a two-thirds majority of the vote would be needed to stop them changing the College position to non-opposition; following vigorous protestation, this was massaged downwards to a mere 60 per cent.

The result showed (again) that the largest proportion of members (43.4 per cent) wanted the RCP to maintain its opposition to assisted dying. But the 60 per cent figure to stop the change was, inevitably, not reached. The percentage supporting assisted dying increased from 24.6 per cent in 2014 to 31.6 per cent, while a quarter preferred that the RCP remain neutral.

'With a virtually guaranteed outcome, this is a sham poll with a rigged outcome,' wrote the former chair of the College's own ethics committee, while the current chair, Professor Albert Weale, resigned over the issue, along with two other members (so far). Undaunted, the RCP has declared its new position: it is no longer opposed to 'assisted dying', it is 'neutral' on the issue and henceforth will not engage in public debate.

And so another medical body has flipped on assisted dying by dropping its long-standing opposition. The means may have been extraordinary, but the outcome is common. Even though the World Medical Association and the American Medical Association recently rejected rather more conventional attempts to change their anti-euthanasia positions, the number of medical bodies no longer opposed steadily rises. The list now includes the Royal College of Nursing in the UK, the Canadian Medical Association, the American Academy of Family Physicians and the state medical organisations in California, Oregon, Vermont and Massachusetts as well as other professional bodies around the world. It is true that bills to legalise assisted dying have been rejected in Britain, South Australia, and the American states of New Mexico, Maryland, Arizona, Arkansas and Virginia, and furthermore that American state referendums have more commonly failed than succeeded. But the sheer volume of physician-assisted suicide bills (PAS bills were rejected in 27 states in 2017 alone) is a measure of the pressure under which the historical position of opposing the practice is now subjected. Assisted suicide is now legal in eight US states (soon to be nine with the addition of New Jersey), and in Canada, the Netherlands and Belgium, Luxembourg, Switzerland, Germany and Colombia. In Australia, legalisation will come into effect in the state of Victoria in a few months.

But 25 years ago, not a single one of these legislatures or medical associations supported assisted dying. Indeed, the only organisations in favour were the Voluntary Euthanasia Society in Britain and the Hemlock Society in the US (now respectively Dignity in Dying and Compassion & Choices). Clearly euphemisms work. Indeed, 'assisted dying' itself is a relatively recent term for 'physician-assisted suicide' (PAS)– or more brutally, to paraphrase Lord Bingham, assisting in killing: 'There is no substantial moral distinction of principle between assisting someone to kill themselves (assisted suicide) and killing them with their consent as in voluntary euthanasia.'

'I will use treatment to help the sick... but never with a view to injury and wrong-doing. Neither will I administer a poison to anybody when asked to do so, nor will I suggest such a course.'

Hippocrates

In PAS, doctors prescribe and provide, and if necessary help administer, lethal drugs to those patients whose wish for suicide we approve of, with the deliberate intent to cause their deaths. Doctors carry on attempting to rescue those whose wish for suicide we deem unsatisfactory (the majority, at least so far), even if that is explicitly against the patient's wishes.

When so articulated, the arbitrariness and subjectivity, and hence the dangers and the unsustainability, of the concept become apparent – as they have been since the ethics of medicine were first considered. Hippocrates saw no need for neutrality on euthanasia. He swore: 'I will use treatment to help the sick... but never with a view to injury and wrong-doing. Neither will I administer a poison to anybody when asked to do so, nor will I suggest such a course.' Swearing by Apollo (not to mention Asclepius, Hygieia and Panacea) might rankle with even the less progressive among us, but physician-assisted suicide remains opposed by the World Medical Association, the Declaration of Geneva, the British Medical Association and the American Medical Association. In the UK, more than 80 per cent of those doctors most intimately involved in the end of life – palliative care physicians –are opposed to PAS.

Without going into a detailed discussion of the ethics of PAS, it's fair to say its proponents argue first that individual autonomy trumps all other considerations, including those of society in general and its most vulnerable in particular (ironically, a pseudo-Thatcherite 'me, me, me' position). Second, they insist there is no 'slippery slope', the extension of PAS far beyond those for whose 'benefit' it was initially intended.

But observing the practice where it has formally been adopted longest shows this slippery slope can no longer be dismissed as alarmist, reactionary rhetoric, but has become incontrovertible, documented fact. Originally introduced only for competent, consenting adults who were in the final stages of terminal illness, the list of those deemed suitable for euthanasia now includes infants in the Netherlands, through the rather sinister-sounding Groningen Protocol, by which with vicarious consent, babies who are not terminally ill may be despatched, if a 'poor quality of life is predicted'. Though fear not, all shall be well! – since 'after the decision

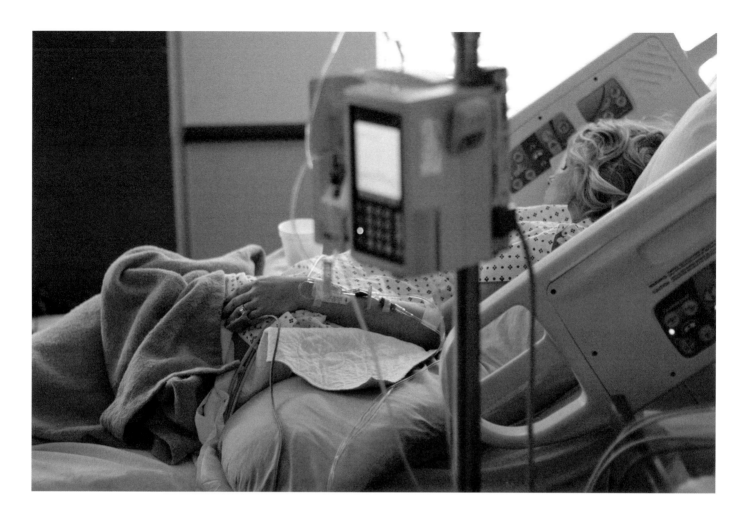

has been made and the child has died, an outside legal body should determine whether the decision was justified'. In Belgium, doctors are authorised to end the lives of children requesting to be killed. But again, the same reassurances! – 'once any euthanasia – for a child or an adult – has occurred, a six-member commission examines the case file to make sure everything was done properly'.

And what of autonomy? Studies a decade ago in the Netherlands reported 400 deaths a year where 'the ending of life [was] without an explicit request by the patient'. In Belgium, where 5% of all deaths are now by euthanasia, 32% of deaths recorded as PAS were 'without explicit request by the patient'. Latterly, the 'service' in several regions has been extended to the demented, the depressed, and even those with Autism Spectrum Disorder and Borderline Personality Disorder.

Indeed, how could it not be so extended? As psychiatrist Mark Komrad has written, 'Principles of justice have made it very difficult to limit such procedures to [one] category

> **'Another bad argument is that the frail will be intimidated into hastening the end of their lives so as not to be a burden on their children. Well, why not?'**
>
> **Polly Toynbee,**

of people... It is unjust, and therefore impossible, in a democratic society, to limit these procedures to some – like the terminally ill – but refuse it to others – like those with chronic physical and psychiatric disabilities.'

No group is more alarmed by these trends than the disabled – physically, intellectually or psychologically. The clamour in favour of assisted suicide telegraphs a message, to quote the prominent ethicist Daniel Sulmasy, of 'social sanction of the idea that lives characterised by incontinence, cognitive incapacity, and dependence on others are unworthy of life and so can be ended by direct killing'. In Britain, the wheelchair-using Baroness Campbell wrote: 'Disabled peoples' lives are invariably seen as less worthwhile than those of non-disabled people.' This is hardly paranoia – witness the unguarded writings of journalists such as *The Guardian*'s Polly Toynbee: 'Another bad argument is that the frail will be intimidated into hastening the end of their lives so as not to be a burden on their children. Well, why not?' Or philosophers such as the late Baroness Warnock: 'If you are demented, you are wasting people's lives, your family's lives, and you are wasting the resources of the National Health Service.' The annual data report published since Oregon passed its Death With Dignity Act shows a marked increase in the number of people citing fear of becoming a burden on family, friends or caregivers as a reason for seeking death – from just over one-third in the first five-year period, to nearly two-thirds by 2018.

As to the RCP's new stance of 'neutrality', both ethicists and physicians point out that it is untenable. Doctors are central to PAS: they are both judge and (forgive the metaphor) executioner. Daniel Sulmasy and Baroness Finlay, professor of palliative medicine, recently wrote: 'Professions have a positive ethical responsibility to take public stances on issues that are central to the meaning of their work. Neutrality on PAS, in this light, seems an abdication of professional responsibility. Doctors helping patients to kill themselves is either problematic, or not.

These changes matter. They have impact. As Dr William Toffler, professor of family medicine in Oregon and a GP for 35 years, has written, 'Since the voters of Oregon narrowly legalised physician-assisted suicide 20 years ago, there has been a profound shift in attitude toward medical care – new fear and secrecy, and a fixation on death.' When various jurisdictions legalise the procedure, and influential bodies drop their opposition, society is influenced.

'Popular indifference, justification by experts and elites, judicial sanction and legislative endorsement change the cultural view of life... This is no slippery slope. This is the way cultures change,' wrote Jeffrey Riley, professor of ethics at New Orleans Baptist Theological Seminary.

The recent muddled reporting of the sad death of a Dutch girl with a history of rape, PTSD and severe anorexia is informative. Initially paraded by many media outlets as

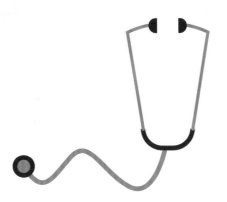

another euthanasia death, subsequent reports indicated that her formal request for euthanasia (at the age of 16, and unbeknownst to her parents) had in fact been rejected. Rather, she was allowed to die at home having for days or weeks refused food and water. For many, the issue is not the initial mis-reporting, but a culture that now permits the suicidal death of a deeply-troubled 17-year-old by voluntary stopping of eating and drinking. (Another bleak outcome was that the Dutch euthanasia clinic named in the 'fake news'–the Levenseindekliniek– subsequently reported a surge in calls from individuals requesting euthanasia.)

The Royal College of Physicians, and other 'neutral' bodies, argue that their position accommodates the varied opinions held by members–though there is no other policy issue on which the RCP has required unanimity, none even where a 'super-majority' has been required.

'To change from opposition to neutrality represents a substantive shift in a professional, ethical, and political position, declaring a policy no longer morally unacceptable; the political effect is to give it a green light.' Certainly, this is how such a change is perceived in the press – 'RCP no longer opposed' was a standard headline. The pro-euthanasia groups find both encouragement and ammunition in medical bodies' abandonment of opposition, and society is changed. By fair means or foul, the tide now appears to flow clearly with the assisted suicide lobby.

26 June 2019

Can we be trusted with euthanasia?

As Belgium shows, it doesn't take long for a nation to normalise death on demand.

By Ian Birrell

It is largely accepted in the modern democratic world that people have the right to do as they determine with their bodies and their lives. We permit competent adults to make many important choices such as sleeping with whom they want, altering their appearance with cosmetic surgery, having an abortion or changing gender. Many things that were once taboo have rapidly become normalised.

So should we let individuals make the ultimate decision: to control the timing and nature of their own death when they have debilitating and terminal health conditions?

This question cuts to the heart of our humanity and rights. Several places in North America and Europe already permit death-on-demand in different forms. Now, as pressure grows for reform in the UK, often driven by powerful testimonies from terminally-ill people, the influential Royal College of Physicians is polling its 35,000 members on whether the law should be changed. The body has said it will ditch its opposition to any change unless six in ten doctors are opposed.

For Britain to follow Belgium, Canada and the Netherlands down the path towards euthanasia, would be significant. Our nation is seen as a pioneer in the creation of the hospice movement and development of palliative care thanks to the late and very great Dame Cicely Saunders. But surveys indicate there is strong public support for change. I am, as an atheist and unashamed liberal, philosophically sympathetic to those seeking legalisation of assisted dying.

Yet, ultimately, I am concerned about any proposed change. Putting aside my admiration for our palliative care system, which I have seen at first hand within my own family, this is for two key reasons. The first was driven home to me two months ago when I spent a few days investigating the impact of this issue in Belgium.

This was the world's second nation to legalise euthanasia and almost 15,000 people have officially ended their lives this way since 2002. It was impressive to see how assisted dying had become entwined within health and palliative systems. Beyond those with strong religious beliefs, I found few concerns over people with late-stage cancer or the cruellest physical conditions opting to terminate their lives. Some doctors remained uneasy about killing patients themselves with fatal doses of drugs, yet were content to assist people who had made rational choices to end their own lives. Other medics were more sanguine, such as the activist doctor I met who had personally despatched 140 people including two of his own friends.

Yet there is no doubt that in Belgium there is a slippery slope: as euthanasia becomes normalised in medicine and society, the number of cases surges and the scope widens. Look also at the Netherlands, where assisted dying now accounts for one in 25 deaths and right-to-die activists are pushing for 'tired of life' legislation that would permit any elderly person over a certain age to obtain drugs to kill themselves on demand.

'The process of bringing in euthanasia legislation began with a desire to deal with the most heartbreaking cases – really terrible forms of death,' the ethicist Theo Boer, a member of a Dutch regional euthanasia board for nine years, was quoted as saying in *The Guardian* last month. 'But there have been important changes in the way the law is applied. We have put in motion something that we have now discovered has more consequences than we ever imagined.'

Belgium, for example, now permits euthanasia for children. It has allowed at least three minors – two of whom were children under 12 – to receive lethal injections since the law was changed five years ago. It also allowed a pair of deaf adult twins who feared turning blind to kill themselves. And it is available for those with 'unbearable' psychiatric pain. If we accept people have the right to death as relief from intense suffering, then this makes ethical sense, since there should not then be distinction between physical and mental agony. Yet such distress is harder to detect and more open to subjective interpretation.

It can also be highly complex. One woman scientist told me she felt more comfortable and in control of her life once she had been permitted to choose her own time of death, and experts pointed out that euthanasia is kinder on a patient and their family than the grisly alternative of suicide. Yet it is hard not to be unsettled when you hear, as I did, the tale of a depressed woman aged only 21 going through a legal process that will end in death. I also heard concerns from psychiatrists over elderly people facing pressure to kill themselves; in at least one case, simply to enrich their family.

It is, therefore, no coincidence that both Belgium and the Netherlands face landmark court cases over controversial deaths following this surge in numbers. One involves the diagnosis with autism of a 38-year-old woman, the other concerns the disturbing incident of an older woman with dementia who had to be held down by her family as she struggled during her final injection.

Which leads me to my second cause for concern: how do we protect vulnerable people once the state starts sliding inevitably down that slippery slope towards the place where euthanasia becomes routine?

It seemed incredible that an autism diagnosis could trigger a euthanasia decision. I discovered a quartet of British and Dutch professors who also had serious concerns, having reviewed cases of people with autism spectrum disorders or learning disabilities who were granted euthanasia. As these experts pointed out, feelings of isolation and an inability to participate in society had come to be deemed as 'unbearable suffering', the legal requirement for ending a life. 'Suffering was described in terms of characteristics of living with an autism spectrum disorder,' according to one of their papers, 'rather than an acquired medical condition.'

This is a terrifying glimpse of how society fails such people – something that chills me to the core as father of a young woman with profound learning disabilities. Surely the real cause of their suffering was the lack of support that might enable them to live contentedly with their conditions, compounded by the woeful lack of acceptance of people who view the world differently which still stains so many societies.

Back in Britain, I have been investigating how hundreds of people with autism and learning disabilities are locked up in horrific and unsuitable psychiatric units. This barbarism includes being slammed in solitary confinement, fed like animals through hatches and on the floor, forcibly injected with powerful drug cocktails, and even children violently restrained by teams of adults. Remember that Belgian scientist I spoke to who was in such mental pain she was granted euthanasia? Her troubles, she told me, went back to when she was held in similar conditions as a teenage girl – yet still we incarcerate scores of teenagers today in the same way, wrecking their lives.

Private operators have moved in like vultures in Britain to exploit this trade in incarcerating human beings, while politicians make empty pledges to end such disgusting abuse. Health secretary Matt Hancock is only the latest to express horror and then kick the issue into the long grass. Sadly, this symbolises again how citizens with autism and learning disabilities are seen as lesser people – along with all the continuing abuse, the hate crimes, the bullying in residential homes, the school exclusions, the dearth of jobs and far too many early deaths in the health system.

So, yes, I remain sympathetic to the concept of assisted dying for those with chronic conditions. But as I have seen in Belgium, once the door is opened, it does not take long for a nation to normalise death on demand. And while I'm not anxious on moral grounds, I do fear for the safety of the most excluded people in society. Until our country shows it respects the human rights of all its inhabitants, then we simply cannot be trusted to handle such a potentially lethal reform.

1 February 2019

Legalise assisted dying for terminally ill, say 90% of people in UK

Opinion poll shows growing support in Britain for change to law on right to die.

By Owen Bowcott, Legal Affairs Correspondent

More than 90% of the UK's population believe assisted dying should be legalised for those suffering from terminal illnesses, according to an opinion poll that shows growing support for change to the law.

A survey carried out by the campaign group My Death, My Decision (MDMD) also found that 88% of respondents considered it acceptable for dementia sufferers to receive help to end their lives, provided they consented before losing their mental capacity.

The results have been released as the Royal College of Physicians polls its members this month on whether they back a change to the ban on the right to die. The Channel Island of Jersey has launched a review on whether to introduce assisted dying legislation.

The MDMD poll was conducted by the National Centre for Social Research (NatCen) and involved 2,500 respondents. A previous survey carried out by Dignity in Dying in 2015 found that 82% of people supported assisted dying.

Providing medical assistance to end a life is legal in Belgium, Canada, Colombia, Holland, Luxembourg, Switzerland and seven US states. The UK Assisted Dying Coalition has collected figures showing that more than one person a week now travel from Britain to Switzerland to end their life.

The two most recent legal challenges to the UK ban have been dismissed by the courts, which ruled that it was up to parliament to decide on the issue. Last November, the supreme court turned down an application to hear a claim from lawyers for Noel Conway, a retired lecturer who is paralysed from the neck down by progressive motor neurone disease.

The previous month, a father of three, identified only as Omid T, who was suffering from a severe neuro-degenerative condition, had travelled to a Swiss clinic to end his life. Five days after he died, the high court ruled against his legal challenge.

Helping someone kill themselves is a criminal offence that carries a maximum sentence of 14 years and is prohibited by section 2(1) of the Suicide Act 1961. Euthanasia is considered murder under UK law.

The MDMD survey asked respondents whether it would be correct to allow assisted suicide in a number of circumstances. It found that 93% of the public would consider medical help acceptable in some situations, including when the person is suffering from an incurable illness that will eventually cause their death.

The organisation's chief executive, Dave Osmond, said: 'These results show that the gulf between our politicians and the public is widening, as assisted dying becomes increasingly acceptable. Time and time again we have told our decision-makers that the right to choose the manner and timing of your own death is a fundamental human right. Yet, time and time again, their inaction has let down families like my own.

'I will never forget the courage of my mother-in-law when she asked me to help her go to Switzerland. Nor the agony I and my entire family went through, by having to choose between helping her, and risking imprisonment, or not and watching her continue to suffer.'

Osmond was questioned by murder squad detectives after accompanying his terminally ill mother-in-law to the Swiss clinic. 'It was a traumatic experience,' he said. 'Each case has to go before the director of public prosecutions. Eventually, they decided no further action should be taken.'

Alex Pandolfo, a supporter of MDMD who suffers from Alzheimer's and who expects to travel to Switzerland to end his life, said: 'Dementia is a cruel disease, and has slowly robbed my life of its quality. Even the basic things, such as planning to see friends, reading, or going outside alone, have become impossible now. In place of the freedom and independence I used to enjoy, my life has now become full of fear.

'If I waited until I had six months left, not only would I no longer have capacity to make that decision, I'd be forced to live, for potentially years, as the very antithesis of the person I am now.'

Parliament last voted on assisted dying in 2015, rejecting by 330 against to 118 a private member's bill to legalise assistance for those who were terminally ill and likely to die within six months.

Unlike some other right to die organisations, MDMD does not believe assisted suicide should be restricted to only those who are terminally ill with a prognosis of six months or less.

The campaign group Care Not Killing opposes the right to die and argues that the law should not be changed. Responding to the supreme court's ruling on Conway last autumn, it said: 'The judges, parliamentarians, doctors and disability rights groups are all in agreement – that the safest law is the one we currently have. It carefully balances an individual's rights with the need to protect vulnerable people, who could feel pressured into ending their lives.'

3 March 2019

Assisted dying case 'stronger than ever' with majority of doctors now in support

By Paul Gallagher

The case for assisted dying is 'stronger than ever', according to the *British Medical Journal (BMJ)* as a new poll reveals most UK doctors support it.

A survey of 733 medics on doctors.net.uk found 55 per cent agreed or strongly agreed with the proposition. Some 43 per cent were against assisted dying and two per cent had no opinion.

> *'The current disconnect between BMA policy and the views of doctors and patients undermines the BMA's credibility, and its continuing opposition excludes it from the public debate.'*
>
> Jacky Davis, Consultant Radiologist, Whittington Hospital London

The poll, which ran for ten days last October, asked whether doctors agreed that assisted dying should be made legal in defined circumstances. The number of doctors who responded is more than double the 313 British Medical Association members who voted on BMA policy at its 2016 annual meeting.

Yet the BMA, which represents UK doctors, has long been officially opposed to assisted dying, despite calls for it to adopt a neutral stance.

Disconnect

Jacky Davis, consultant radiologist at the Whittington Hospital in London, who is also a member of BMA Council, a board member of Dignity in Dying, and chair of Healthcare Professionals for Assisted Dying, said: 'The current disconnect between BMA policy and the views of doctors and patients undermines the BMA's credibility, and its continuing opposition excludes it from the public debate.'

Writing in the *BMJ* among a series of articles on the debate, Ms Davis said 'assisted dying does not represent a leap into a dangerous unknown', citing other jurisdictions, such as the US state of Oregon, where next month will be the 20th anniversary since it introduced an assisted dying law.

'Predictions of systemic abuse and inevitable broadening of eligibility criteria have not come true,' she writes. 'Ultimately legalisation for assisted dying will be a decision for UK society.'

In a linked commentary, Bobbie Farsides, professor of clinical and biomedical ethics at the University of Sussex, argued that palliative care and assisted dying are not mutually exclusive.

'Patients are more aware than ever of what is, and is not, possible for them as they approach the end of their lives, and practitioners need to be prepared and able to respond compassionately,' she says.

Rather than fighting against a possible future in which dying people could get medical help to die, she urges health professionals 'to think about how they would negotiate such a future in the the best interests of their patients'.

Sarah Jessiman, a patient living with terminal cancer, explains why she thinks doctors should support the campaign to legalise assisted dying in the UK.

'I'm terrified of the sort of death I may have to face,' she writes. 'I would draw huge comfort from knowing that I could say 'enough' when I can no longer endure my illness, so I can die at home, supported by the people I love most. I don't want to go to Switzerland, and I don't want to attempt suicide. Why can't I die as I live – in an open and honest way?'

However, Bernard Ribeiro, a retired surgeon and life peer, argues that assisting suicide would damage trust between doctors and patients and 'is a matter for the courts, not for the consulting room'.

Editorial support

Dr Fiona Godlee, editor in chief of the BMJ, said the journal supports an assisted dying law.

'The great majority of the British public are in favour and there is now good evidence that it works well in other parts of the world, as a continuation of care for patients who request it and are in sound mind,' she said. 'We believe that this should be a decision for society and parliament, and that medical organisations should adopt at least a neutral position to allow an open and informed public debate.'

> *'This not a new poll, its questions were narrowly framed and it is being promoted by a journal that does not represent the medical profession.'*
>
> Dr Peter Saunders, Campaign Director, Care Not Killing

Dr Peter Saunders, campaign director of Care Not Killing, said: 'This not a new poll, its questions were narrowly framed and it is being promoted by a journal that does not represent the medical profession and has become almost fanatical in its support for changing the law to allow doctors to kill their patients.

'A change in the law is opposed by every major disability rights organisation and doctors' group, including the BMA, Royal College of GPs and the Association for Palliative Medicine, who have repeatedly looked at this issue in detail and concluded that there is no safe system of assisted suicide and euthanasia anywhere in the world.

7 February 2019

Majority of Scots back 'assisted dying'

By Kevan Christie

Nearly nine in ten people in Scotland support legalising assisted dying, according to a new poll.

The Populus survey, commissioned by campaign group Dignity in Dying Scotland, found 87 per cent backed the move for terminally ill people with less than six months to live, with medical approval and safeguards.

Just eight per cent of people were opposed while the remainder said they did not know.

The results, from a survey of 1,057 adults last month, were released as the campaign group starts a national advertising drive calling on people to help legalise assisted suicide.

Campaigners want the Scottish Parliament to legislate to allow terminally ill, mentally competent adults to have the choice of an assisted death.

People with terminal illnesses who back assisted dying and those who have lost loved ones who would have chosen the option if it were legal in Scotland feature in the campaign.

Liz Wilson, 45, from Cumbernauld is one of those taking part.

Her husband Craig died from cancer in December and she said had 'begged' to go to Switzerland where assisted dying is legal but was unable to travel.

She said: 'Craig was only 45 when cancer took over his whole body. It was horrific to watch him suffer in the way he did. No amount of palliative care could help him.

'For Craig, while he was dying a minute was like an hour and a day like a year. He begged to go to Switzerland but it was sadly too late.'

She added: 'I don't believe anyone should have to go through what Craig did. I have promised to campaign to change the law so no-one else has to.'

Dawn Morton, 34, from Dunfermline also features in the campaign.

She was diagnosed with motor neurone disease in 2014 and now needs 24-hour ventilation and care.

Ms Morton wants to be able to choose assisted suicide to spare her six-year-old daughter Abigail from watching her die in pain.

She said: 'I couldn't afford to go to Switzerland and it is important to me to be around as long as possible for my daughter, but I don't want her to see me die badly and in pain.

'I wish the choice of assisted dying was available in Scotland so I could decide when the time was right for me.'

Dignity in Dying Scotland director Ally Thomson said: 'Most Scots believe that dying people should not be forced to suffer at the end of life and that there are currently too many bad deaths.

'Their views cannot be ignored. The law in Scotland needs to change.'

She added: 'This campaign is all about love and putting the voice of people who have lived and are living through the injustice of the current law at the heart of the debate.'

A cross-party group of nine MSPs recently joined together to call for assisted suicide to be legalised in Scotland.

Previous attempts to change the law at Holyrood have failed.

Chief executive of the Care Not Killing umbrella group opposing assisted suicide, Gordon Macdonald, said: 'The last time MSPs voted on the issue of assisted suicide, they rejected Patrick Harvie's Assisted Suicide Bill by 82 to 36.

'Most members realised then that the risks of legalising assisted suicide were too high and would put vulnerable people at risk of harm to justify taking that step.'

He said instead of 'encouraging suicide' more money should be made available for palliative care.

2 April 2019

www.scotsman.com

Nearly half of GPs would want assisted death, poll suggests

By Laura Donnelly, Health Editor

Almost half of GPs would want to be prescribed drugs to help them die if they were terminally ill and suffering unbearably, a poll suggests.

The survey of more than 1,000 family doctors found most would want the option of 'assisted dying' under certain circumstances.

The poll, commissioned by a pressure group in favour of assisted dying, comes as the Royal College of Physicians questions its members on its position.

The College has been accused of running a 'sham poll' by medics who say that it has framed the survey in order to shift its position.

Currently the RCP's position opposes assisted dying.

But the terms of the survey state that it will adopt a neutral position, unless there is a 60 per cent majority for or against.

Previous polls found 44 per cent said the college should be formally opposed, with 31 per cent backing a neutral stance, and 25 per cent wanting it to support assisted dying.

A free vote in the Commons in 2015 rejected proposals that would have allowed people with less than six months to live to be prescribed drugs to end their lives with the approval of two doctors and a judge.

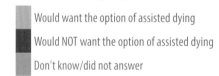

GPs were asked: 'If you were terminally ill and suffering unbearably at the end of life with only months or weeks to live would you personally want or not want the choice of assisted dying in order to control the manner and timing of your death?'

- Would want the option of assisted dying
- Would NOT want the option of assisted dying
- Don't know/did not answer

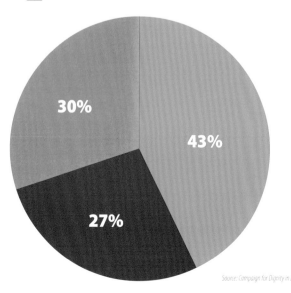

30%

43%

27%

Source: Campaign for Dignity in Dying

John Saunders, a former chairman of the college's ethics committee, has threatened a judicial review of the poll, saying it is 'manifestly unreasonable' that if it delivers the same result as a 2014 vote it will change the position.

The new poll of GPs was commissioned by Campaign for Dignity in Dying, which is calling for a change in the law to allow assisted dying.

It found that 55 per cent of GPs said medical bodies should adopt a position of neutrality on the issue of assisted dying for terminally ill, competent bodies.

The survey, carried out by research company medeConnect, also asked family doctors what they would want for themselves.

GPs were asked: 'If you were terminally ill and suffering unbearably at the end of life with only months or weeks to live would you personally want or not want the choice of assisted dying in order to control the manner and timing of your death?'

In total, 43 per cent said they would want the option of assisted dying , while 27 per cent said they would not. The remainder did not know or chose not to answer.

Dr Jacky Davis, Chairman of Healthcare Professionals for Assisted Dying, said: 'These results show what we know to be true, that there's no consensus amongst doctors when it comes to the subject of assisted dying. Because of that, most doctors think their medical colleges and representative bodies should adopt a neutral stance so that everyone's views can be represented.'

The results of the poll by the Royal College of Physicians will be released next month.

Professor Andrew Goddard, RCP president, said: 'The Royal College of Physicians is frequently asked for its stance on this high-profile issue, which may be cited in legal cases and parliamentary debate, so it is essential that we base this on an up-to-date understanding of our members' and fellows' views.

'Because doctors are divided on the issue, the RCP wants to ensure that we only hold a position one way or another if there is a clear majority view. If the vote is for a neutral position this would mean that the RCP neither supported nor opposed a change in the law, and could reflect the differing views of its members. This should not be taken to mean support for a change in the law to allow assisted dying.'

5 February 2019

What's really beneath the assisted dying debate?

Andrew Grey argues that by meeting people's needs and wishes at the end of their lives, professionals enable them to have dignified deaths.

'Dignity' in death is for many people associated with assisted dying. When the US state of Oregon legalised assisted dying, the law was entitled the 'Death with Dignity Act' (1997). The Swiss clinic where people famously have gone for an assisted death is named 'Dignitas'.

Here in the UK, assisted dying is currently illegal, despite the attempts (most recently by Lord Falconer and Rob Marris MP) to propose a change in the law. If dignity means the choice of assisted dying, it would seem to follow that dignified death is either impossible, or at least rare, in the UK.

Yet many people in the UK do have dignified deaths, at least according to the doctors, nurses and chaplains who care for them at the end of their lives. We interviewed a number of these professionals for our new report, *Dignity at the End of Life: What's Beneath the Assisted Dying Debate?*

What made the deaths of those they cared for 'dignified'? For the professionals we spoke to it was, above all, that people felt valued: in the words of one consultant, 'knowing you're loved as you go'.

These professionals showed people they were valued in the way they communicated with them – listening to them and caring about their lives. An essential part of this was supporting the people who mattered to them, such as their friends, families and partners, but it was also seen in the way they cared for them. This included doing everything within their power to meet people's needs and wishes for the end of their lives, such as having their pain and other symptoms managed, their spiritual needs being met, and, as far as possible, being at peace.

The professionals saw valuing people as part of honouring their dignity as human beings. This affected the approach they took to caring for the person. It meant listening to people's concerns, and treating them with the basic dignity most of us would want – especially when they were afraid of being humiliated.

When potentially uncomfortable situations arose, such as incontinence, or being washed, professionals spared their humiliation as far as possible. This included practical measures such as using continence products, but also recognising where the person felt uncomfortable and helping reassure them that their symptoms were simply part of their illnesses, and not something to feel ashamed of.

By meeting people's needs and wishes at the end of their lives, these professionals enabled them to have dignified deaths. Doing this required investment – in time, patience and resources – but it sent a clear message to people that they matter.

This message stands in stark contrast to that of people who feel that assisted dying is an efficient alternative to the costly

and burdensome option of caring for people until they die naturally. This isn't a 'straw man'. Indeed, it was a point made by one of Britain's leading moral philosophers, Baroness Mary Warnock, in 2008, about people with dementia. For Baroness Warnock, if you have dementia, 'you're wasting people's lives – your family's lives – and you're wasting the resources of the National Health Service', and may even have a 'duty to die'.

Of course, not everyone who advocates assisted dying does so for this reason – in fact, many people don't. But what begins as a law change to enable a minority to have this wish granted could trigger a gradual change in culture, whereby terminally ill people who feel they are a burden consider assisted dying a duty.

True dignity at the end of one's life does not consist in making a choice of when and how one dies. If we are really to honour people's dignity, we must care for them and the people who matter to them and do all we can to ensure they are at peace, and have their wishes and care needs meet. In doing so we can send terminally ill people a clear message that, in the words of Dame Cicely Saunders (founder of the modern hospice movement) – 'you matter because you are you, and you matter to the end of your life'.

1 February 2018

www.theosthinktank.co.uk

Assisted dying debate: 'My husband begged me to help him die'

By Kirsteen Paterson

Liz Wilson knows love, and she knows death. She went through both with her husband Craig, who died in a hospice less than a year ago.

The stay-at-home dad, 45, died in December after an aggressive form of cancer spread through his body, robbing him of almost all functions in his final days.

All he had left at the end was pain, thirst and love for his family.

Liz, from Cumbernauld, said: 'We didn't want Craig to go. He loved his life, he loved his daughter, but palliative care isn't always enough.

'He was only in the hospice for two months, but it was too long. It was far too long. We say you wouldn't let an animal suffer, what about people? He used to say, "Why can't I go to sleep and die?". At times he would be begging to go.'

Liz is one of several Scots involved in the Dignity in Dying campaign, which is calling for a law change to allow adults in the last stage of their life to end it.

The campaign wants the Scottish Parliament to make the provision for people with terminal illness and the mental capacity to take the decision, subject to checks by doctors.

The provision sought would not allow anyone to end another person's life, something campaigners say would act as a safeguard to ensure all assisted deaths are carried out voluntarily.

Liz says if the law had already been changed, it would have spared her family, including teenage daughter Jennifer, the trauma of Craig's death, and some of the most heart-rending conversations the couple ever had.

Now undergoing counselling, she recalls how 'gentle giant' and keen gamer Craig would ask her to find a way to end his constant pain, telling her: 'You need to figure out a way to do it.'

She said: 'He was always so thirsty. I researched it and told him he could stop taking his water. He said, 'I can't stop the water.' I said, 'I know darling, you're already suffering enough. Do you know how many times I thought about pinching your nose and putting my hand over your mouth when you're asleep?' I'd want somebody to do it to me.

'He said, 'No, you've got Jennifer'.

'People that love each other the way we did should never have been put in a position to have that conversation.

'That's criminal, because it is a compassion.'

Those conversations took place after doctors ruled out the option of assisted death in Switzerland's Dignitas clinic.

'I promised I'd be his voice in death.'

While Craig wanted to go there, his condition had progressed to the point that travel was not possible.

What he went through, and what the extended family went through, has left Liz with a burning anger. On her involvement with Dignity in Dying, and the Scottish Parliament's rejection of earlier attempts to change the law, she said: 'It's the fury that's driving me on.

'I want to shout from the rooftops what Craig went through and what we as a family witnessed.

'I relive it when I talk about it now, but I'm giving Craig a voice.

'I was his voice in the last few weeks because he couldn't communicate – I could tell from his body language if it was pain relief or water he needed.

'I promised I'd be his voice in death.'

Craig died in his wife's arms, and she washed and laid out his body. She said: 'There was no-one on this Earth loved more than Craig. Everyone loved him, we were soulmates.

'It was like Daddy Day Care at our house – all the kids in the street would come in to play with Jennifer and he'd run about making them all toasties and juice and set them up on their computer games.

'He was a homebody, and he was very private. He felt humiliated by the personal care he had to have, it was so embarrassing to him, even though the nurses were great.

'The hospice was great, but there's only so much palliative care can do. Their hands were tied.

'We didn't realise what we were facing. He'd been told there would be pain relief and they'd keep him comfortable, but he was in pain and he wasn't comfortable. He tried acupuncture, everything. At the end his head turned to the right and he couldn't move it. After he died I found a bed sore on his ear and that really upset me.

'Life is precious, but so is quality of life. I respect other people's opinions and I know there are people who don't want this as a choice, but it is a choice – we're not saying we want assisted dying for everyone, that we want everyone to do it. It would give people who need it the option.

'If you don't want to use assisted dying, don't use it. But don't deny other people the choice to end their suffering.'

14 October 2019

Terminally ill man denounces assisted dying law after police interview wife over his plan to die at Dignitas

'The law in this country robbed me of control over my death,' Geoffrey Whaley tells MPs in letter published as he ends life in Swiss clinic

By Chris Baynes

A terminally ill man whose wife was interviewed by police over his planned death at a Swiss clinic has called for urgent changes to the UK's assisted dying laws.

In an open letter to MPs published minutes before he ended his life at Dignitas, accountant Geoffrey Whaley said his final months had been 'blighted' by visits from social services and a criminal investigation.

The 80-year-old, from Chalfont St Peter in Buckinghamshire, arranged to die at a clinic near Zurich after he was diagnosed with motor neurone disease in 2016.

His wife Ann, 76, supported his wish to avoid a protracted death but faced the threat of prosecution after an anonymous tip-off to Thames Valley Police.

'As I was saying my final goodbyes and preparing myself for the end, the final, biggest bomb dropped and I could no longer keep it together,' Mr Whaley said. 'Within hours Ann and I were facing a criminal investigation. The thought that I might not make it to Switzerland, or that, if I did, Ann might be facing 14 years in jail for helping me, was almost too much to bear.'

Mr Whaley had booked into the Dignitas clinic himself but asked his wife to arrange flights and a hotel in Switzerland after losing the use of his arms in the final weeks of his life.

Police interviewed Ms Whaley under caution twice before informing her she would face no further action.

In his letter, Mr Whaley told MPs: 'I want to impress upon you the anguish me and my family have experienced, not because of this awful illness, but because of the law against assisted dying in this country. The law in this country robbed me of control over my death. It forced me to seek solace in Switzerland. Then it sought to punish those attempting to help me get there. The hypocrisy and cruelty of this is astounding.'

Mr Whaley ended his life at 10am on Thursday. He was surrounded by his wife, his children Alix and Dominic, and close friends.

Speaking before the family travelled to Switzerland, Ms Whaley said: 'Geoff and I have been very happily married for 52 years. I have never seen him cry. The day the police called, he sobbed. In my eyes, I am not a lawbreaker; I simply love my husband.'

At least three Britons have faced a criminal investigation after returning home from a loved one's assisted death overseas, although none have been prosecuted.

More than 170 people have travelled from Britain to die at the Dignitas clinic in Switzerland in the last five years.

The process costs an average of £10,000, according to Dignity in Dying, which campaigns for changes to the UK's assisted dying law.

Sarah Wootton, the organisation's chief executive said: 'Banning the practice in this country does not make it go away; it simply outsources death overseas, at huge financial, practical and emotional cost to the families involved.'

British MPs last voted on assisted dying in 2015, when they rejected proposals to allow some terminally patients end their lives with medical supervision by 330 votes to 118.

Opponents of assisted suicide argue it would be open to exploitation and patients could be coerced into ending their lives prematurely, but supporters of law change say in-built safeguards could protect the vulnerable.

79% of the British public believe assisted dying should be legalised, according to a YouGov poll published this week.

7 February 2019

By the time you read this, I will be dead

An open letter to all MPs from Geoffrey Whaley. Written before his death at Dignitas.

Dear Members of Parliament,

By the time you read this, I will be dead.

On Thursday 7th February 2019, I will have taken medication that will end my life, surrounded by my wife, Ann, my children, Alix and Dominic, and a couple of my dearest friends at the Dignitas facility in Switzerland. With their love and support I have been able to fulfil my final wish: to be in control of my end, rather than endure the immense suffering motor neurone disease had in store for me.

I want to impress upon you the anguish me and my family have experienced, not because of this awful illness (though of course this has been incredibly difficult), but because of the law against assisted dying in this country. The blanket ban on assisted dying has not only forced me to spend thousands of pounds and endure months of logistical hurdles in order to secure a peaceful and dignified death overseas, but it has meant that my final weeks of life have been blighted by visits from social services and police.

Since my diagnosis of MND, an incurable, terminal illness, in 2016, I felt as though bombs have been dropping on me. I gradually lost the use of all four limbs. My ability to speak, swallow and breathe began rapidly deteriorating. I knew my death was inevitable and unavoidable, but I remained strong for my family. I am 80 years old and have lived a full life. I did not fear death, but I did fear the journey. I simply wanted to cut this suffering short by a few months. When I eventually got the 'green light' from Dignitas, a weight lifted; I was able to get on with living without the constant mental anguish over my death.

But then, as I was saying my final goodbyes and preparing myself for the end, the final, biggest bomb dropped and I could no longer keep it together. This bomb was in fact an anonymous phone call to social services who informed the police of my plans to go to Switzerland. Within hours Ann and I were facing a criminal investigation. The thought that I might not make it to Switzerland, or that, if I did, Ann might be facing 14 years in jail for helping me, was almost too much to bear.

'In 52 years of marriage, Ann had not seen me cry. The day we were contacted by the police, I sobbed.'

The law in this country robbed me of control over my death. It forced me to seek solace in Switzerland. Then it sought to punish those attempting to help me get there.

The hypocrisy and cruelty of this is astounding. Though it is perfectly legal for me to make arrangements and travel to Dignitas by myself, the minute anyone else 'assists' me in any way – which is essential, due to my condition – they are liable for prosecution.

I had the chance, just over a week before my death, to speak to some MPs and Peers about my experience and my adamant wish that the law should be changed. The overwhelming reaction in the room was one of agreement; however, I am aware that despite huge public support for an assisted dying law, most members of parliament currently oppose it. I spoke to one MP who had voted against the last assisted dying Bill in 2015. The law being proposed was limited to terminally ill, mentally competent adults in their final months, with strict inbuilt safeguards to protect the vulnerable and anyone else who has not made a clear decision of their own volition. When I pressed her on why she felt people like me should be denied a say over our own death and be forced to suffer, she was unable to articulate an answer.

I want MPs to know that change is urgently needed and that it is achievable – over 100 million people in several American and Australian states and across Canada are covered by assisted dying laws which allow choice to dying people and protection to others. No family should ever have to endure the torment we have undergone in recent weeks, but it will be easier to bear knowing that by sharing it we can contribute to future change. I sincerely hope that you will truly listen to our story and see the suffering you are inflicting by upholding the status quo.

Yours sincerely,

Geoffrey Whaley

Chalfont St Peter, Buckinghamshire

7 February 2019

Geoff's widow Ann is now campaigning with Dignity in Dying for a change in the law on assisted dying.

Dignity in Dying campaigns for a change in the law to allow assisted dying as a choice for terminally ill, mentally competent adults in their final months of life.

www.dignityindying.org.uk

Assisted dying – a personal story

In May 2003, Lesley Close accompanied her brother, who had advanced Motor Neurone Disease, to Switzerland where he chose an assisted death with the help of Dignitas. Here she relates her experience and belief that there is a need for serious debate about the right to die for people with terminal illnesses.

In March 2001 my brother John Close was diagnosed with Motor Neurone Disease (MND) at the age of 53. He had a limp and some difficulty speaking and swallowing. Compared to many victims of what David Niven called 'this bloody awful disease', John's decline was slow.

John was prepared for every diminution of his abilities before I became aware of it. His mobility deteriorated from using a walking stick at diagnosis to having a Zimmer frame by late summer 2001 and he was a full-time wheelchair user by spring 2002. Similarly, his speech went from difficult to understand in spring 2001 through being garbled by autumn 2001 to just a series of aspirations coupled with extraordinary facial expressions by summer 2002. He tried using a Lightwriter but, being very tech-savvy and somewhat impatient, he preferred to use a hand-held machine with a small display I could read quickly.

By Christmas 2002, John needed full-time care. It's easier to tell you what he *could* do at that point than to list what had been taken away from him: he could still wipe his own bottom (provided he used his non-dominant, left hand) and he was able to type (slowly) with the fingers of that same hand. Yes – that's the end of the list. In contrast, his mental capacity was fully intact and he was the same funny creative person he had always been.

It was that massive difference between the life of the mind and the life of the body that dismayed John most about the prospect of letting MND take its natural course to end his life. He didn't want to become what a Christian friend who was diagnosed with MND just under a year after John called being 'a living head on a dead body'. John didn't want to live if he was unable to communicate anything that was going on inside his mind – and there was a lot going on there!

In January 2003, John saw a BBC News item about Reg Crew's trip to Dignitas. He showed me the web story and, after I had read it, typed *That's how I'd like to go when my time comes*. I immediately understood why John wanted an assisted death – it allowed him to choose a death which was guaranteed to be peaceful and dignified.

Opponents of assisted dying with whom I have debated the subject have often suggested that I should have put a stop to John's ambition, that I should not have facilitated his journey to Switzerland. My response is to ask what John would have gained if I had selfishly insisted that he continue suffering until MND ended his life?

Knowing that he would be in control of his death was a tremendous source of comfort for John. Indeed at a stage when MND had almost totally eroded his quality of life, knowing he would have that control gave some dignity back to him. Because I was with John as he died I too have lasting comfort: I know he didn't suffer and I have an abiding memory of him smiling, just minutes before his life ended. John's death was sad but my grief at losing him was tempered by the control he had over the way he died.

Getting to Switzerland wasn't easy, partly because (understandably) the kind and compassionate people at Dignitas don't rush things and we had to ensure we provided adequate proof of John's terminal diagnosis and fit mental state. But on Monday 26th May 2003, a public holiday in the UK, we took an early morning easyJet flight to Zurich. After completing some further paperwork in the Dignitas office, John was taken in to the consulting room of the doctor who had reviewed his application for assistance to die. The two men were alone to start with and, when I was asked to join them, the doctor asked me about John's medical history. He also asked about John's family left at home (there was only our mother, and John didn't have any children) and he made sure that I understood what John was about to do.

And then the doctor said something everyone who opposes assisted dying should consider as they relate to a doctor's duty towards alleviating a patient's suffering. He said: *My main duty as a doctor is to preserve life but, here in Switzerland I have an extra duty. I will perform that duty for you, Mr Close, and write the prescription to help you die.* And with that he left the room. The silence which fell wasn't just due to John's lack of speech – it was the expression of a profound sense that the end of John's suffering was not far away now...

In fact, John died a couple of hours later and a few miles away in central Zurich. Because he was weak and tired, I helped him to connect the drug-filled syringe to his PEG feeding tube. After saying our goodbyes, John pressed the plunger – it is a requirement under Swiss law that the medication is self-administered – and the massive dose of barbiturates went straight in to his stomach. I held his hand as the drug took effect and he fell into a deep sleep. Unconsciousness soon followed and, after twenty minutes, John achieved the peaceful and dignified death he wanted.

But the fact that John's death took place in Switzerland meant that I did not feel peaceful. The first language of everyone we dealt with was not English, our frail and elderly mother could not be with her son for she too was a wheelchair user and, above all, as a newly bereaved person I was adrift in a foreign city.

I also had to prepare myself for the risk of prosecution when I got home. Although ending your own life has not been a crime since the 1961 Suicide Act was passed, assisting a suicide remains a crime and carries a maximum sentence of 14 years. Helping someone to arrange an assisted death in Switzerland or accompanying them there could be interpreted as 'assistance'. I didn't face a police investigation but it remains a risk for the loved ones of those who seek an assisted death overseas.

If medically assisted dying – such as the provision which now exists for over 100 million people in several American and Australian states and across Canada – had existed in the UK in 2003, John might have lived for a few weeks longer. Only weeks, though, as his body was failing fast and he was in danger of having a crystal-clear intellect with no means of expressing himself.

I wish John had been able to die that same peaceful and dignified death at home, at sunset and after his own GP had written the prescription. That GP, Eric Rose, spoke to the British Medical Association a few weeks after John's death and said that knowing John had changed his opinion about assisted dying.

A change in the law to allow assisted dying as a choice for terminally ill, mentally competent adults is something the vast majority of British people want to see. Estimates indicate that, even if there was universal access to hospice care in the UK, seventeen people a day would still die in pain and suffering. At least 300 terminally ill people a year end their lives in England and, because of that ban on assistance with suicide, they have to act alone – how frightening must that be? Every eight days someone from Britain makes the journey to Switzerland simply to have control over the end of their life, a process that costs £10,000 on average.

The UK's blanket ban on assisted dying gives people some stark choices – to suffer against their wishes, to take drastic measures behind closed doors, or to travel overseas and risk criminalising family members who offer compassionate assistance. That's no way to treat people who are suffering intolerably as their lives end.

I believe it is time that politicians stopped pussy-footing around this issue: Dignitas is a marvellous organisation, but we should not be exporting the problem of assisted dying to another country.

5 December 2019

Marieke Vervoort: Belgian Paralympic athlete and advocate of euthanasia

A gold medallist at the London games, she drew attention four years later in Rio with the announcement that she would end her life if her pain became unendurable.

By Christine Manby

In 2012, Belgian athlete Marieke Vervoort took gold in the 100m T52 wheelchair class at the 2012 Paralympic Games in London. Unbeknownst to the crowds who cheered her on to victory, Vervoort had already made the decision that would bring her to worldwide attention again four years later. Just prior to the Rio games she announced that when the pain caused by the degenerative spinal condition that had put her in a wheelchair became unendurable, she would end her life by euthanasia.

Vervoort, who has died aged 40, was born in Diest to Jos and Odette Vervoort. She was 14 when she first noticed the symptoms of what would be diagnosed seven years later as reflex sympathetic dystrophy, a degenerative condition of the spine and muscles. A keen sportswoman who excelled at basketball and loved diving, she suddenly found herself able only to walk using crutches.

Soon Vervoort had lost the use of her legs altogether, but she was determined not to let disability keep her from the sports field. She played wheelchair basketball and competed in triathlons. In 2006 and 2007 she was paratriathlon world champion. As her condition continued to deteriorate, Vervoort was no longer able to compete as a triathlete, so turned her attention instead to blokarting and wheelchair racing.

Vervoort's determination soon had her back at the top of her field. At the 2012 Paralympics, she set a European record time for the T52 100m wheelchair race of 19.68 seconds, beating Canadian Michelle Stilwell. She also took home silver in the T52 200m. A year later, she set a European T52 200m wheelchair race record, which was followed by world records in the T52 400m and the T52 800m. Her unstoppable success earned her the nickname 'the Beast from Diest'.

Vervoort's 2013 record-breaking roll met an abrupt end when she badly injured her shoulder in a collision with her Paralympic rival Stilwell during a race at the IPC Athletics World Championships in Lyon. She was warned that she should not expect to race at such a high level again, but Vervoort defied the medical advice and came back to compete at the Para Athletics IPC Grand Prix in Switzerland less than a year later. There she took gold in the 200m and set new world records in the 1,500m and the 5,000m. In 2015, at the IPC Athletics World Championships in Doha, she took three more golds and was crowned world champion.

In 2016 at the Rio games, Vervoort won two medals, a silver and a bronze, despite having spent the day prior to winning silver in the T52 400m on a rehydrating drip after she was struck down with vomiting bug. But she knew that Rio would probably mark the end of her competitive career.

Prior to the games, Vervoort had publicly revealed for the first time that she was considering euthanasia. Assisted suicide has been legal in Belgium since 2002 and it was in 2008 that Vervoort signed the papers that would allow her to make the choice when the time came.

Vervoort said it was a liberating decision that actually made it easier for her to carry on, knowing she could end her life on her own terms. In an interview three months after her success at Rio, she told Radio 5's Eleanor Oldroyd: 'If I didn't have those papers, I wouldn't have been able to go into the Paralympics. I was a very depressed person – I was thinking about how I was going to kill myself… It's thanks to those papers that I'm still living… With euthanasia, you're sure that you will have a soft, beautiful death.'

Having given up wheelchair racing, Vervoort took up indoor skydiving. An assistance Labrador named Zenn helped her to maintain a level of independence at home. In addition to helping Vervoort dress and fetching items she needed, Zenn was also able to sense when an epileptic seizure was imminent – sometimes up to an hour before it happened – and warn Vervoort to find a safe space to lie down. But by 2017 Vervoort was spending much of her time in hospital. Her eyesight had deteriorated, sleep was elusive, and she was in constant pain.

Vervoort planned her funeral in meticulous detail. She told Eleanor Oldroyd, 'I wrote to every person who's in my heart… I wrote texts that they had to read. I want that everybody takes a glass of cava [and toasts me] because she had a really good life. She had a really bad disease but thanks to that disease, she was able to do things that people can only dream about… I want people to remember that Marieke was somebody living day by day and enjoying every little moment.'

Marieke Vervoort, Paralympic athlete, born 10 May 1979, died 22 October 2019

9 November 2019

We need to talk about how assisted dying affects doctors

By Nancy Preston

This week the High Court will hear the case of Noel Conway on whether he can receive a 'medically assisted' death.

Key to that request is the word 'medically'. Much of the debate around assisted dying focuses on the person asking to be helped to die. The public assume that if legal then this would become part of the health system, with the patient's doctor being involved. When Terry Pratchett discussed the Bill to make assisted dying legal in the UK once again he discussed it in terms of 'having one's life ended by gentle medical means'.

'Hospitals don't want to be seen as death factories.'

But this raises the question: what is the impact on medical professionals when assisted dying becomes legal?

A legal vacuum in Switzerland

There are different forms of assisted dying around the world. People are most familiar with Dignitas in Switzerland where, although assisted dying is not legal, there is no punishment in assisting someone to die, so some doctors do it. In Switzerland this is called physician-assisted suicide. The doctor prescribes drugs which the patient takes themselves to end their life.

In lieu of legislation, the Swiss Medical Academy have developed guidelines to support doctors, but the doctors know they are acting in a legal vacuum. The image of assisted dying as part of mainstream medicine in Switzerland isn't the case – assisted deaths in hospital a rarity.

Our research has shown hospitals don't want to be perceived as death factories, and sometimes discharge patients specifically so they can have an assisted death. Virtually no palliative care doctors in Switzerland will prescribe the necessary drugs, leaving people to seek help from right to die associations.

Swords hanging over doctors in the Netherlands

In the Netherlands where both physician-assisted suicide and euthanasia is permissible, there is a clear legal system to support this work by doctors and some cases do occur in healthcare settings.

In contrast to physician-assisted suicide, euthanasia is where the doctor administers an injection directly to the patient. Interestingly there are very low rates of physician-assisted suicide in the Netherlands but increasing rates of euthanasia. We don't know why this is. Is it because the doctor administers the lethal injection meaning it can be carried out much later or because the doctor performs the act themselves which somehow sanitises it? Although legal, for each doctor the case will be examined by authorities and their role evaluated – leaving doctors potentially feeling

> **Physician-assisted suicide:**
> A doctor supplies drugs which a patient can use to end their life.
>
> **Euthanasia:**
> A doctor injects a patient with lethal drugs to end their life.

they have the sword of Damocles hanging over them until cleared.

'Though doctors agree people should have the choice to end their lives, some decide that they can't perform the act themselves'.

Some doctors opt out altogether but they may still be involved in the patient's care. If a doctor doesn't want to prescribe the lethal injection can the relationship with the patient be maintained? A survey showed the overriding feeling of doctors after an assisted death was one of relief but these same doctors felt greater relief after a natural death.

Some doctors feel regret

Of those who assist patients, research shows some feel regret afterwards. We also know it takes a toll on them. Even though they agree people should have the choice, some decide over time that they can no longer perform the act themselves. As one doctor said, 'It's not good for me.' They refer to it being a heavy burden and say they can only be involved in a couple of cases a year.

The burden of being asked to perform euthanasia became too much for another doctor who moved away to a different job to avoid being asked. Others are more comfortable but they agree it is never a normal death, and they remember each one. We know even less about the impact to the wider healthcare team.

The public desire that doctors should be involved could be asking too much of some. Whatever happens in the UK, doctors need training and support in how to deal with their own reactions to these cases.

Dr Nancy Preston is a Senior Lecturer in the International Observatory on End of Life Care at Lancaster University. She is involved in research about palliative care including trying to understand the impact of assisted dying in society including a new study interviewing relatives of people from the UK who have used Dignitas.

20 July 2017

Key Facts

- Assisted suicide is illegal under the terms of the Suicide Act (1961) and is punishable by up to 14 years' imprisonment. (page 1)

- In the Netherlands both euthanasia and assisted suicide are legal if the patient is enduring unbearable suffering and there is no prospect of improvement. Anyone from the age of 12 can request this, but parental consent is required if a child is under 16. (page 4)

- Belgium, Luxembourg, Canada and Colombia also allow both euthanasia and assisted suicide. (page 4)

- A study published in 2009 using responses from more than 3,700 medical professionals suggested 0.2% of deaths involve voluntary euthanasia and 0.3% involved euthanasia without explicit patient request. (page 5)

- It is legal in the UK for patients to refuse treatment, even if that could shorten their life. (page 5)

- Figures from Switzerland show that the numbers of those living in the country who underwent assisted suicide rose from 187 in 2003 to 965 in 2015. (page 5)

- In the Netherlands there were 6,585 cases of voluntary euthanasia or assisted suicide – 4.4% of the total number of deaths. (page 5)

- According to statistics from Dignitas, 221 people travelled to the country for this purpose in 2018, 87 of whom were from Germany, 31 from France and 24 from the UK. (page 5)

- 93% of people in the UK approved of, or wouldn't rule out, doctor-assisted suicide if the person is terminally ill. (page 6)

- People generally support the idea of doctors ending the life of a terminally ill person who requests it (78%), but that there is less support for a close relative doing the job (39%). (page 6)

- The Forfeiture Act 1982 lays down a simple rule that an individual cannot benefit from someone's death if they have 'unlawfully aided, abetted or procured' the death. (page 14)

- In 2014, polling showed that when people were presented with the five key arguments against legalising assisted suicide, support dropped dramatically to below 50%. (page 21)

- In Washington State, where 56% of those who died under the Death with Dignity Act said they were concerned with being a burden on family, friends or caregivers. (page 21)

- Belgium was the world's second nation to legalise euthanasia and almost 15,000 people have officially ended their lives this way since 2002. (page 26)

- In the Netherlands, assisted dying now accounts for one in 25 deaths. (page 26)

- More than 90% of the UK's population believe assisted dying should be legalised for those suffering from terminal illnesses. (page 28)

- 88% of people consider it acceptable for dementia sufferers to receive help to end their lives, provided they consented before losing their mental capacity. (page 28)

- Euthanasia is considered murder under UK law. (page 28)

- 93% of the public would consider medical help acceptable in some situations, including when the person is suffering from an incurable illness that will eventually cause their death. (page 28)

- Parliament last voted on assisted dying in 2015, rejecting by 330 against to 118 a private member's bill to legalise assistance for those who were terminally ill and likely to die within six months. (page 28)

- A survey of 733 medics on doctors.net.uk found 55 per cent agreed or strongly agreed with the proposition. Some 43% were against assisted dying and 2% had no opinion. (page 29)

- Nearly nine in ten people in Scotland support legalising assisted dying, according to a new poll. (page 30)

- Almost half of GPs would want to be prescribed drugs to help them die if they were terminally ill and suffering unbearably, a poll suggests. (page 31)

- At least three Britons have faced a criminal investigation after returning home from a loved one's assisted death overseas, although none have been prosecuted. (page 34)

- More than 170 people have travelled from Britain to die at the Dignitas clinic in Switzerland in the last five years. (page 34)

- The process to end a life at Dignitas costs an average of £10,000. (page 34)

- 79% of the British public believe assisted dying should be legalised. (page 34)

Active euthanasia

Active euthanasia is deliberately intervening to end someone's life – for example, by injecting them with a large dose of sedatives.

Advance decision

Sometimes referred to as 'living wills', advanced decisions are legal statements outlining a patients wishes with regards to their medical treatment should they not be able to make decisions or communicate their wishes at a later stage. Advanced decisions can include the request for life-sustaining or life-prolonging treatments, as well as the refusal of treatments.

Assisted dying

Assisted dying allows a dying person the choice to control their death if they decide their suffering is unbearable. It is illegal in the UK.

Assisted suicide

Aiding somebody to take their own life. This is illegal in the UK.

Autonomy

The ability to make independent, informed decisions, free from coercion or outside influences. It is sometimes argued that patients should have greater autonomy over their medical treatment and the freedom to choose euthanasia if they wish.

Dignitas clinic

A clinic in Switzerland which assists terminally-ill patients to end their lives. Non-medical assisted suicide is legal in Switzerland and terminally-ill patients from other countries sometimes travel to the clinic specifically to end their lives. This is sometimes referred to as 'death tourism'.

Disability

The Equality Act 2010 defines a disabled person as anyone who has a physical or mental impairment that has a substantial and long-term adverse affect on his or her ability to carry out day-to-day activities (NHS Choices, 2012). The nature of the disability will determine the extent to which it impacts on an individual's daily life. The definition of disability includes both physical impairments, such as multiple sclerosis or blindness, and learning disabilities such as autism.

Double effect

The principle of double effect refers to a treatment prescribed by a doctor for the purpose of relieving pain or distressing symptoms, but which has the side-effect of shortening the patient's life. Although the doctor will be aware that the treatment will induce an early death, it is not considered euthanasia because the main reason for the prescription is pain relief.

End-of-life care

This refers to the health and social care received by adults who are approaching the end of their lives. Some critics of an assisted dying law suggest that if end-of-life care in the UK was of a higher standard, fewer people would seek to end their own life when terminally ill.

Euthanasia

The practice of ending a life to relive pain and suffering.

Involuntary euthanasia

Intentionally ending a patient's life without their consent. Even if the act of euthanasia is motivated by compassion it is still considered involuntary euthanasia if the patient in question is unable to give informed consent.

Palliative care

A specialist area of care which provides relief from pain but does not cure a disease or illness. It is often administered to patients suffering from terminal illnesses in order to improve their quality of life before they die.

Palliative sedation

The sedation of a terminally-ill patient in order to relieve suffering and pain. This option is considered a last resort and is only used in the final moments of a patient's life.

Passive euthanasia

Passive euthanasia can be causing someone's death by withholding or withdrawing treatment that is necessary to maintain life.

Physician-assisted suicide (PAS)

A doctor prescribing lethal drugs in order that a patient may take their own life is known as physician-assisted suicide.

Sanctity of life

A term usually associated with religious faiths, particularly Christianity, which refers to the idea that all life is sacred as created by God, and no human being has the right to end a life.

Slippery slope argument

One of the principal arguments given by anti-euthanasia groups and individuals. The 'slippery slope' argument suggests that if a government were to legalise voluntary euthanasia, a change in citizens` and healthcare professionals attitudes would eventually result in implications such as involuntary euthanasia, pressure on very ill or disabled people to end their lives prematurely and a decline in the importance placed on palliative care.

Terminal illness

An illness for which there is no cure and which will ultimately bring about the patient's death.

Voluntary euthanasia

Intentionally ending the life of a patient who has previously given their consent for euthanasia. It is usually requested by patients who are suffering from a terminal illness and who wish to end their pain and suffering.

Will

A legal document made by a person before their death, containing instructions about matters such as funeral arrangements and division of property in the event of their death.

Activities

Brainstorming

- In small groups, discuss what you know about euthanasia. Consider the following:
  - What is assisted suicide?
  - What is euthanasia?
  - What is assisted dying?
  - Is there a difference between assisted suicide and euthanasia?
  - What does UK law say about assisted suicide?
- In small groups brainstorm either for or against euthanasia. Include as many ideas as you can.

Research

- Research euthanasia laws in the UK and compare them to countries in Europe. Summarise your findings and share with the rest of your class.
- Conduct a survey amongst your friends, family and classmates to explore peoples' opinion about assisted dying. Write a summary of your findings and illustrate with graphs and charts.
- Research end-of-life care in the UK. What are the options for people who are terminally ill? What issues have been raised in the media? Make notes on your findings and share with the rest of your class.
- Choose a religion (different to your own beliefs) and research their thoughts on euthanasia.

Design

- Choose one of the articles from this topic and create an illustration that highlights the key themes of the article.
- Design a poster that explains the current laws about assisted suicide in the UK.
- Create a poster that depicts a map of the world and illustrates assisted suicide laws in different countries.
- Choose one of the articles in this book and design an infographic to represent the themes of the article.
- Create a PowerPoint or Prezi presentation arguing either in favour of or against the legalisation of euthanasia in the UK.

Oral

- As a class, debate euthanasia. Half of the class should be for and half against.
- In pairs, discuss the potential negative consequences of legalising assisted suicide in the UK.
- In pairs, choose one of the illustrations from this topic and discuss how the artist has depicted the key themes/messages of the article it accompanies.
- What is 'physician-assisted suicide'? Discuss in small groups.
- In pairs, discuss whether you think that people with terminal illnesses should be able to choose to end their own life or not.

Reading/writing

- Write a one-paragraph definition of euthanasia..
- Write a letter to your local MP arguing either in favour or against a change in the assisted suicide law.
- Why do you think someone might choose to end their life at the Dignitas clinic? Explore your answer to this question in no more than 500 words.
- Using newspapers and the Internet, carry out your own research into a legal case which has influenced public opinion and/or the law with regards to the assisted suicide debate. What did those seeking a change in the law hope to achieve, and why? What conclusion did the courts reach? Do you agree with the conclusion? Write a summary of your findings.
- Watch *Me Before You* (2016) or read the book. Write a diary entry from both Lou and Will's point of view. How do you think they will differ?
- Read 'Tetraplegic model speaks out against euthanasia after once planning to end her life' and 'Marieke Vervoort: Belgian Paralympic athlete and advocate of euthanasia' and compare and contrast the two articles.

Acknowledgements

The publisher is grateful for permission to reproduce the material in this book. While every care has been taken to trace and acknowledge copyright, the publisher tenders its apology for any accidental infringement or where copyright has proved untraceable. The publisher would be pleased to come to a suitable arrangement in any such case with the rightful owner.

Images

Cover image courtesy of iStock. All other images courtesy of Pixabay and Unsplash, except page 22 kjpargeter from Freepik.com

Illustrations

Don Hatcher: pages 18 & 37. Simon Kneebone: pages 11 & 26. Angelo Madrid: pages 8 & 12.

Additional acknowledgements

Page 15: The copyright in the document this publication has been adapted from and all other intellectual property rights in that material are owned by, or licensed to, the Commission for Equality and Human Rights, known as the Equality and Human Rights Commission ("the EHRC")

With thanks to the Independence team: Shelley Baldry, Danielle Lobban, Jackie Staines and Jan Sunderland.

Tracy Biram

Cambridge, January 2020